THE
CASE
FOR
DUAL
LOYALTY

Healing the Divided Soul
of American Jews

NOLAN LEBOVITZ

WICKED SON

A WICKED SON BOOK
An Imprint of Post Hill Press
ISBN: 979-8-88845-853-2
ISBN (eBook): 979-8-88845-854-9

The Case for Dual Loyalty:
Healing the Divided Soul of American Jews
© 2025 by Nolan Lebovitz

Cover Design by Jim Villaflores

Scripture quotations are taken from The Jewish Publication Society (JPS) and Sefaria. Used by permission. All rights reserved.

JPS Hebrew-English Tanakh the Traditional Hebrew Text and the New JPS Translation. 2nd ed. of the New JPS translation. Jewish Publication Society, 1999.

Koren Talmud Bavli. Commentary by Rabbi Adin Even-Israel (Steinsaltz). Koren Publishers, 2012.

Translations are the author's own but they are derived in conjunction with these sources.

This book, as well as any other Wicked Son publications, may be purchased in bulk quantities at a special discounted rate. Contact orders@posthillpress.com for more information.

Published in cooperation with the Z3 Project. For more information visit Z3Project.org.

WICKED SON

Post Hill
PRESS

Post Hill Press
New York • Nashville
wickedsonbooks.com
posthillpress.com

Published in the United States of America

*And Moses said to the tribes of Gad and Reuben,
"Will your brothers go to war inside
the Land while you live here?"*

Numbers 32:6

CONTENTS

INTRODUCTION

This moment of challenge for American Jews should prompt us all to reconsider our choices. Thousands of years of decisions made by millions of our ancestors—individually and collectively—have led to this moment. There are many ways to understand the maelstrom of Jew-hatred that has engulfed college campuses, media, and pro-terror rallies around the country. Our leaders scramble to explain it as a reaction to geopolitics, a rise of populism, a rise of anti-Americanism and anti-Western ideologies, a reflection of political hyper-polarization, or a reorientation of social alliances.

This book will not seek to explain or remedy antisemitism.

As the historian Gil Troy pointed out in the *Jerusalem Post* in June 2024, the problem of Jew-hatred cannot be solved by Jews. "This isn't a fight about Israel and Palestinians; it's about democratic values…," he writes. "Jew hatred is the disease of Jew-haters, not Jews." Antisemitism in America will have to be addressed by government, law enforcement, and supportive American neighbors of all religious and ethnic backgrounds. We can certainly work to understand this ancient hatred more honestly, but we cannot rectify it. Just as the heart cannot resolve heart disease, Jews cannot resolve Jew-hatred.

My focus lies on the soul of the American Jew. What American Jews *can* do is begin making different choices to strengthen our Jewish identities. Indeed, we must reorient ourselves to a Jewish practice that prioritizes different values than before.

For too many decades, American Jews—and especially liberal Jews who constitute the majority—have overemphasized "Tikkun Olam" Judaism, a social-justice effort to repair the world around us. Social justice, however, is easy. It does not often require much education to appreciate. Social justice feels rewarding, and it fits within the contemporary context of intersectionality: American Jews can feed the homeless alongside Methodists and Muslims.

We must continue Tikkun Olam programming, but we now see that it provides a false sense of belonging to a greater universal effort—while frequently diminishing the particular nature of the Jewish people and the unique bonds Jews share with one another.

It is time to reorient American Judaism. Our defining American Jewish mission must be to cultivate our sense of peoplehood. There are times in our history that demand that we reexamine our choices that have led to our current standing. This is one. We must see our fellow Jews as our family, as our priority.

I am a Jew grateful to have been born and raised here in America. I pledge allegiance to our flag of the United States of America. I also recognize my shared connection with Jews everywhere. The Jewish people is my ancestry, and it's my extended family. As part of the Jewish people, I maintain a loyalty to the Jewish state, the State of Israel. Israel is the embodiment of our people—and comprises a large portion of it, as well.

Jews in America and across the diaspora now have to make a choice to summon a stronger connection to the Jewish people—and, by extension, to Israel. We must choose to define ourselves as *no less loyal to our people than to our host nations.* Loyal to both.

Such a dual loyalty is nothing to be ashamed of. In fact, our collective Jewish soul depends on it.

~

"Death to the Jews!" is a recurring refrain in history. It has been a rallying cry for those who stand against intellectuality, those who stand against progress, those who stand against classical liberalism. Whenever we hear it, darkness, demagoguery, and death are never far behind—for everyone, not just the Jews.

We can hear the refrain gaining traction once again.

Jeering crowds have chanted it before. If you listen carefully to the whispers of time, you can hear it in a range of dialects and accents from Assyria to Babylonia, from Spain to Germany, from Iran to South Africa. For the first time in my life, I can hear the chant across American cities. It has arrived in a variety of forms, including a new variant: an anti-colonialist, pro-terror slogan, "from the river to the sea!" This cry advocates for a Palestinian state to displace the entire State of Israel—including all of its Jewish population—from the Jordan River to the Mediterranean Sea. Over time, the words might change, but the bloodthirsty sentiment remains the same.

How should we respond? Or, rather, how might we respond differently to pave for ourselves a better collective Jewish future?

We must begin by examining our past. As Jews, we walk in a tradition of previous generations with whom we live our lives, from whom we learn important lessons, and thanks to whom we transmit unique teachings. We interact with our past and future on a regular basis through our learning, our holidays, and our sacred day of rest, Shabbat. We must learn from our past, because although the threat of Jew-hatred remains, the answer for this moment must be crafted as a suit of armor of Jewish identity moving forward.

One of the most iconic examples of this kind of mob demand for Jewish blood took place in Paris in 1894. A decorated French artillery officer named Alfred Dreyfus stood accused of treason. Dreyfus's impressive military accomplishments carried no weight. Because, as a Jew, he stood in the place of the eternal scapegoat. Crowds exhibited their Jew-hating mania through chants and signs. French media conjured up tropes that smeared Jews at large. Served up on a platter, Dreyfus stood no chance. Convicting him in 1895, the court publicly humiliated him and stripped him of his rank. Following his verdict and degradation, Dreyfus professed his loyalty: "I swear that I am an innocent man. I remain worthy of serving in the military. Long live France!"

In our bones, we all know what he was doing. We've been raised to do the same. His attempt to push back by affirming his own credentials as a good citizen feels logical. His desire to prove that a Jew should be considered an equal, a Frenchman, is a learned internalized behavior that has resulted from generations of abuse at the hands of Jew-haters. As Charles Darwin might argue, the instinct of Dreyfus reveals a survival skill developed by thousands of years of diasporic evolution. It is a daunting task to unlearn survival skills. Standing at the center of the storm, he lacked the perspective to chart a new course forward for himself or his people. Luckily, there was such a Jew with perspective observing the trial.

An assimilated Hungarian-Austrian Jewish journalist named Theodor Herzl, who was covering the trial, watched in shock. How could enlightened, liberal French society champion such vitriolic Jew-hatred? Instead of chanting "Death to the traitor!" or "Down with Dreyfus!" the Parisian crowd heckled, "Death to the Jews!" Amid a sea of antisemitic hatred, Herzl could not believe how the French crowd had smeared a loyal military officer of their own. Dreyfus had devoted his life to defending French values; French society viewed him as merely a Jew.

Herzl observed all this like a scientific experiment. He concluded that there is more that connects French Jews and Austro-Hungarian Jews than connects French Jews to French non-Jews. He felt the profound bond of Jewish peoplehood. Herzl determined, "In vain we are loyal patriots."

The response of Dreyfus, to answer the accusation, is the reaction of most Jews. *They say I can't be loyal, so I'll profess my loyalty. They say that I can't be a member of this organization and be a Zionist, so I'll reject my Zionism.* This kind of capitulation serves only the bully. The submission validates the hatred. We can no longer behave this way.

Herzl's reaction guided us in a new direction. Rather than simply answering the accusation, he gave birth to modern Jewish political nationalism, also called Zionism. A sense of our peoplehood will lead one to Zionism, and Zionism will steer one toward our critical value of Jewish peoplehood. Only a short while later, he produced a brief treatise that changed our Jewish historical trajectory: *The Jewish State*, published in 1896. The lessons of nineteenth-century France—from Napoleon through Dreyfus—inspired Herzl, and indeed a significant portion of world Jewry, to build a movement for self-determination in our ancestral homeland. In 1948, Zionism ultimately led to the birth of a Jewish nation-state, the State of Israel.

Zionism has had many miraculous successes over the decades. Yet, Zionism maintained two basic assumptions that have proven false. First, with the establishment of the Jewish State, Zionists expected that the Jewish nation would be able to stand on equal footing with the rest of the nations of the world. As a people, we sought no longer to suffer from isolation or harsher expectations. Nevertheless, Israel continues to be singled out and held to a standard that no nation could ever achieve.

Second, many Zionists expected that with the establishment of Israel, there would be a massive ingathering of Jews from across the world—even to the point of the diaspora's dissolution. This turned out to be only partially true: Over three-quarters of a century, waves of immigration from the Middle East, North Africa, the former USSR, and elsewhere turned Israel into home for a plurality of the world's Jews, but a large diaspora, mostly in the United States, still maintains a robust sense of Jewish life.

Israel's establishment did not break the two-millennium-old tradition of Jew-hatred. It did not break the tradition of diaspora. It will not. Yet, amid antisemitic waves that followed October 7, I believe that it is incumbent on Jews in the diaspora to reassess the nature of our own Jewish identity.

In every other aspect of identity today, we acknowledge the multiple layers of social associations such as religion, gender, sexual preference, socioeconomic status, citizenship, and even sports team allegiance. We must now apply those same lessons to loyalty.

~

The phrase *dual loyalty* will raise an alarm for many readers, and perhaps even engender anxiety. It felt dangerous even to broach the subject, yet in this moment we must reconsider all paths forward. For most of modern history, the term "dual loyalty" has been used as an accusation by antisemites to charge Jews with having ulterior motives. Antisemites may use this book to prove the point. They will always find ways to hate us.

Put aside the hate for a moment. This argument is not about them. It's about us.

We can no longer respect our outdated shibboleths. We need to find new ways to strengthen our sense of self and to craft a brighter tomorrow. American Jews today need not behave like the timid immigrant generation of our grandparents or great-grandparents.

I want to be clear: Ardently, Zionist Jews are sincere, loyal citizens in every diasporic nation-state in which we reside. American Jews are loyal Americans, who have achieved status in the public and private sphere and success in almost every walk of life. We love America. True, we can be loyal American patriots without loyalty to Israel. However, the concept of a singular devout nationalist loyalty serves us no more.

My entire life experience points me to this argument. I inherited my Jewish identity from my family. I am the grand-child of four survivors of the Holocaust, or Shoah. I am the son of first-generation Americans who are ardent Zionists. I am the product of the great American Jewish institutions of the last half century, including Solomon Schechter Day School, USY, and the AEPi fraternity. For the two most formative decades of my life, those institutions helped shape my Judaism. The resulting desire to understand our ancient texts drove me to the Ziegler School of Rabbinic Studies at American Jewish University, my doctoral program in religion at Claremont Graduate University, where I focused on the Hebrew Bible, and my Fulbright Scholarship at Bar Ilan University in Israel.

Throughout my time at each of these institutions, my teachers always encouraged me to think critically about texts, historical narratives, and behavior. Yet, they insisted that there must always remain basic working assumptions for critical thought. I know that in this work, I challenge a basic working assumption for American Jews. We know the danger and the loaded nature of dual loyalty. And yet, I believe this moment calls on us to challenge our assumptions.

Now that I serve as the senior rabbi of Valley Beth Shalom in Los Angeles, one of the great synagogues of consequence in America, I have seen the reactions of a large, multigenerational community to the aftershocks of October 7. One of the lessons is that American Jews had been living in a delusional fantasy about our protected place in this country. From high school to college students, from new professionals to established careers, every American Jew had to open their eyes. As Bari Weiss eloquently stated, the American-Jewish "holiday from history is over."

Those of us raised within the incubator of Jewish institutional life, surrounded by prolific Jewish educators of all types, and familiar with the canon of our tradition, must stop and wonder: Now that our eyes are open, how should we live our lives differently? Which basic assumptions have betrayed our worldview and misled us to believe our position in America to be safer than it really was?

We must begin to carry ourselves differently in order to meet our new challenges in the diaspora. As a student of Judaism, religion at large, history, Jewish texts, Zionism, and rational critical thought, I, for one, am ready to suggest this divergence from more than two centuries of mainstream assimilationist Jewish perspective.

———

The underlying case for dual loyalty that follows will weave together evidence from our current challenges, previous historical frameworks, personal experiences, and biblical portraits, just as we do in creating our modern Jewish identity. For there is no separation between the biblical narrative and our modern narrative, Jewish history, and our lived experience. Ours is a multigenerational drama constantly yearning to learn the lessons of our existence. We are poised again, right now, for a shift in realization.

The instinct of many of the Jews I know is to protect their children from this harsh reality all around us. It is a healthy parental behavior. I wouldn't find this effort so problematic if I didn't feel that in doing so, adults are also trying to shield themselves from this new bitter reality.

With great intention, I try to force my children to hear and see the rallies marching through major cities and esteemed college campuses. I want them to see the obscene hatred in the possessed eyes of the protestors. I want my children to understand that there is no way for us to change them. The protestors might tire or lose interest. The mobs might even be persuaded to stop by paying a price for the brazen antisemitic filth they spew in public. There might be a pause, a cessation. Ceasefire does not end a conflict. It only prolongs it. The hatred will lie directly under the surface. There is no way to unsee what we've seen.

Some already advocate for understanding "complexity" and call for efforts to hold "safe spaces" for conversations between interfaith groups where there are no wrong answers and only personal truths. This is an effort to return to the world of October 6. But, in fact, there *are* wrong answers.

It's wrong to perpetrate the barbaric, heinous acts of October 7. Full stop. The contextualization of the evil of

October 7—the murder, rape, infanticide, looting, pillaging—does not exhibit nuanced thought, but rather complete moral confusion. More and more, too many Jewish leaders are willing to sit down and consider the massacre of October 7 within the Israeli and Palestinian narrative, to reflect on the rise of Jew-hatred as a reaction to Jewish success and over-representation. Habit encourages us to accommodate a backward-thinking world in which the only appropriate response to Jew-hatred is to explain its unjustified nature. That is the logic of Dreyfus.

Modern American Jews have to collectively decide: Are we Dreyfus?

The tragedy of Dreyfus is the unwavering Jewish belief in the Other: Our outspoken loyalty even after having been scapegoated, our devotion to the decency of all humans even when confronted with evidence to the contrary, our unwillingness to change with the changing reality around us.

So, how do we react if there is no way to change them? We must change ourselves. We have to reconstruct our conception of the diasporic Jew.

Only days after October 7, many began to discuss Israel's need to change its *conceptzia* of defense, its relationship with Hamas, and its attitude toward the Palestinians who support them. Israelis understood that they needed a new strategy in dealing with Iran. There is no doubt that the review of data and circumstantial pressure will force Israel to make difficult choices to reset its relationship with the outside world. In the end, I profoundly believe that Israel will be fine.

I am concerned, however, for us: Jews in the diaspora. We also need a new framework for understanding Jewish identity moving forward, especially in America. For the purposes of Jewish survival and continuity, it is paramount that we maintain a thriving Jewish community here. This will prove more and more difficult as the version of America that opened its doors to our grandparents and granted opportunity to our parents declines.

Why do I raise this alarm at this moment? I fear that many misunderstand the brutal Hamas massacre of October 7, 2023, as the generational trauma of our people. I understand October 7, 2023, as the harbinger of the generational trauma of our people.

As shocking as October 7 proved, we have seen the brutal massacre of Jews before. We could not have imagined the aftershocks of October 7. October 8 and beyond hover as an ominous cloud over American Jewry.

To use an analogy that I first heard from Bret Stephens, the Hamas attack against Israel and the reactions throughout the world didn't just mark the presence of the cancerous Jew-hatred we've now seen erupt around the world. The Hamas attack revealed to us, like a CAT scan, that the cancerous Jew-hatred has metastasized to the brain of the civilized world. The central nervous system of this country is at grave risk as its universities, media, and even elected officials have normalized Jew-hatred. Simply put, what I now realize after October 7 is that antisemitism is now completely socially acceptable in America. As a student of history and a Jewish leader, I have to sound the alarm.

October 7 was an inflection point in our Jewish experience here in America. What's our next step as American Jews? I am not alone in raising this question. Many thinkers have begun contemplating this dilemma through conversations and articles. Now, I add my voice to all of theirs.

This argument will feel challenging to most American Jews. Many will feel inclined to close this book quickly. As a child of the 1980s and 1990s, I was raised to believe in American exceptionalism. Further, I believed in a sense of American Jewish exceptionalism. The stories of previous diasporas need not apply to these spacious skies, these amber waves of grain. It took me a long time to wrestle with the question of whether it was even possible for America to head down the path of Germany, Spain, England, Rome, Babylonia, Egypt, and other great civilizations. It already has.

America's decline is real. Its turning on its Jews has begun in earnest. They go hand in hand. Can we push back and alter the current course? Is there a cultural and spiritual and political answer that we can make for ourselves that will help strengthen our Jewish identity at this moment to help fuel this much-needed optimism?

The answer is proud dual loyalty. We must begin to acknowledge the untold truth that has existed amongst most of us since 1948: We are loyal to America, and we are loyal to the Jewish people—and that, by definition, means a loyalty to Israel. This is an important admission for our Jewish souls as we prepare for the future. I have felt this way my entire life, but it wasn't until after October 7 that I felt the need to articulate it to others.

⁓

The idea for this book came one Saturday morning as I sat in front of my congregation. Like so many American Jewish synagogues, ours proudly features an American flag and an Israeli flag in the front of the sanctuary. Those symbols speak volumes. They are meant to instill within us a pride in our position in relation to both countries. We are in relationship with America and Israel. Those symbols in the sanctuary are meant to teach us about the modern reality that is our American Jewish identity. For the generation that placed those flags, they may not have needed to articulate the symbolism. For this generation today, we need to spell it out.

As dire as our circumstances currently seem, our time in America has not yet expired. America has the ability to shape and reshape its policies. It has always been up to our leaders to look into the future and help us prepare. I believe there are still more chapters to our lives here. But, after seeing what we've seen, we cannot live here in the same way. Some will ask for America to change, for American leaders to change, for American institutions to change. I was raised in a house that taught me that the change I seek must begin within me. The much-needed change we now seek must begin with our own vision.

This book's argument follows a simple logic. If America has become a more shaky home for Jews, then we should examine the symptoms of diasporic decay from previous societies. The first chapter will present the historical patterns of diaspora. Then, we must understand what choices Jews made then and choose a different path. The second chapter will examine the problem of dual loyalty. We must understand why Jews chose to profess their singular loyalty and why we're different today. The third chapter will look at the Jewish "double helix," the interdependent relationship between Jews in Israel and Jews in America. Then, we can choose a different course. The fourth chapter makes the case for dual loyalty as our new path forward.

Underpinning this entire argument is a foundational understanding of the power of our own agency. American Jews have choices. We have the choice to live differently based on our experiences since October 7. It will not be easy. Many American Jews will warn against any public acknowledgment of dual loyalty.

Warning of Jewish diasporic reticence, Theodor Herzl concludes his introduction to his groundbreaking political treatise *The Jewish State* with an ominous warning, "Old prisoners do not willingly leave their cells. We shall see whether the youth whom we need are at our command—the youth, who irresistibly draw on the old, carry them forward on strong arms, and transform rational motives into enthusiasm."

It is difficult to change course after many decades of comfort and complacency, but this moment calls for a robust conversation about initiating change. Our change begins with the way we see ourselves.

I invite you to join me in reimagining our existence here. How do we need to change the way we see ourselves? Can we reimagine how our children are raised and educated to meet the new challenges for Jews in America? How can we avoid further missteps now that we have witnessed our new reality? How do we explain to ourselves and future generations that we did not stand pat, that we began to pivot proactively in the wake of October 7?

There is an answer worthy of our Jewish experience. There is an answer that honors our history. There is an answer that aligns with our values. The answer is dual loyalty.

I am loyal to Israel, and I am loyal to America. I have no problem saying it. If that bothers you, I challenge you to keep reading the rest of my argument. Please be aware, I fully intend on convincing you to join me.

CHAPTER 1

The Historical Patterns of Diaspora

As Jews, we don't like to discuss it, but we all know that previous diasporas have come to an end. Like all forms of life, each previous diasporic society is conceived, develops, thrives, and then expires. To study Jewish history is to hold up a flashlight to the wreckage of all our previous exotic fallen Jewish diasporas that have contributed and produced civilizational achievements for the benefit of humanity. Yet despite the productive, flourishing accomplishments of its Jewish population, each host society eventually chooses to turn on its Jews and ultimately devour itself.

For, when Jews are forced to leave a diasporic society, two things inevitably occur. First, the Jewish population of the fallen diaspora disperses. Stripped of our resources, we look for a new home. Some Jews try to return and settle within the Land of Israel, where there has always lived an indigenous Jewish community. Some, if possible, try to assimilate completely, erasing their Jewish identity entirely. Most, however, leave the collapsed diaspora and try to resettle in other foreign lands within a new diaspora.

The second certainty is that the society that expels its Jews inevitably enters a period of decline that sooner or later turns it into a meaningless relic of its former self, eventually relegated to middle-school history textbooks.

This is one of the great takeaways of Jewish history. Much like the great Jewish literary works of our canon, our history repeats itself. Our tradition encourages us to read the same texts over and over in the hope that we will learn the lessons of our past. Annually, we read the entire cycle of the Torah, the Five Books of Moses. Each Passover holiday, we sit around a table and retell the story of our redemption from slavery in Egypt. We tell and retell these narratives, not only because we need to understand our past, but because we relive the Jewish experience again and again. Our past must inform our present; otherwise, our past will become our present.

I believe that the story of America and its Jewish population is not over. I very much believe in the promise of America. As much as is currently wrong with this country, we still have time to correct, to prepare, and perhaps to begin to reflect collectively on countermeasures to the increasingly corrosive nature of our circumstances. Any process of deep reflection must begin with learning. If we study the roadmap of Jewish experience lived over thousands of years, we will notice that tremors become stronger and stronger until the ground beneath our feet explodes. To understand the sequence of the phases is to better understand where Jews stand today in America and how we had better prepare ourselves for the future.

Many focus on the explosion, the earthquake, without close study of the tremors. Each tremor can be contextualized and explained in its own moment. But, when zoomed out all the way, the tremors all form a clear pattern that points to the downfall of each Jewish diasporic experience.

I will present the pattern handed down to us by our ancestors. Then, I will reflect on final explosions, as I don't believe that we are experiencing a final explosion. I know that this is not a final explosion based on our recent past here in America and through my personal family experience with the previous final explosion that drove my family to immigrate to America. By the end of this chapter, we will appreciate the stages of diaspora. With a sense of historical context, we might appreciate the American promise somehow to be different.

~

A quote often attributed to Mark Twain teaches us, "History does not repeat itself, but it does often rhyme." While the assault of a Jewish student on the Harvard campus does not mirror Kristallnacht and *The New York Times* does not duplicate *Der Sturmer*, each Jewish societal catastrophe that features the mass murder or expulsion of its Jews never presents itself as the earthquake explosion without a series of warning tremors. The tremors always rattle us, always worry us, but they subside. The tremors we currently face will also subside. Then, the next set will arrive. Keep in mind, they always grow in severity over time.

Charlottesville in 2017 was worse than Skokie in 1978. College campuses in 2024 were worse than in 2014. The tremors always return. The truth lies in the tremors.

One of the truths realized (again) for us following October 7 is the profound sense of peoplehood among Jews in the wake of the massacre. We raised money to support the IDF. We traveled to Israel to volunteer in the agricultural space. We continue to bear witness and to listen to the devastating stories of the survivors who faced Hamas and Palestinian brutality and sexual violence.

We possess incredible strength through our peoplehood. So how do we harness it moving forward? As the world turns increasingly intolerant of Israel and Jews, how do we rely on one another to create a more hopeful tomorrow? Well, for the Jewish people, no matter where you live, no matter how devout your practice, no matter whether you belong to a synagogue, there already exists a document intended to guide you. We call it the Hebrew Bible.

The Bible is not a narrative that occurred long ago. It is a guiding document that we consult as we live our experience again and again. Like other sacred documents for other peoples, our Bible presents to us ideas and characters for us to draw lessons and compare against our own choices. But unlike other sacred documents for other peoples, our narratives showcase highly human, flawed individuals who try to make the best choices for themselves and their generation with the information they possess. In this way, our stories invite us to consider ourselves and our own lives against the human lives of the biblical heroes.

To use the biblical narrative as a guide, Genesis and Exodus reveal a six-step biblical cycle of diasporic experience that portrays the progression of tremors into total tragedy. These six steps are an eternal truth of our collective Jewish lived history. First, toward the end of Genesis (Gen. 39:1–45:15), Joseph is forced to descend to Egypt. He ultimately finds acceptance and success there. The rest of his family and all of their descendants, the entirety of the Children of Israel, follow him to Egypt in pursuit of food during a time of widespread famine. This is how all diaspora experiences begin for us. Challenges force us to consider new locations that offer us opportunities that we need at the moment.

Second, we are welcomed and pursue economic opportunities through our acceptance. This phase contains Jewish adaptation. Jacob follows his family into Egypt, and Pharaoh graciously offers the land of Goshen to live and prosper in their family business as shepherds (Gen. 45:16–47:11). As a people, we adjust as newcomers to the foreign land, and we prosper.

Third, in its reaction to our success, the foreign society notices the success and prosperity of the Jewish immigrant group and begins to grow concerned. In a section little noticed by most readers of the narrative, Egyptians sell their property to gain access to food, while Joseph and his family gain wealth during the years of famine (Gen. 47:12–27, Ex. 1:1–7). The end of the third phase of experience marks the peak of Jewish life in any particular diaspora. There is a gradual and often indiscernible transition that occurs in the way that the host society begins to treat its Jewish population.

Fourth, the host society begins to implement new treatment, even formal policies, in dealing with its Jewish population. In the biblical narrative, a new Pharaoh expresses concern about the size and strength of the Jewish community and begins to instate policies that lead toward Jewish enslavement (Ex. 1:8–14). The Jewish community capitulates to this new arrangement as the society feels like home. There is an inherent dangerous self-assurance within our people that no matter the new restrictions, we will have the ability to succeed. It is here that the tremors begin.

During the fifth stage—the explosion—the host society attempts to destroy its Jews. These are the historical dates with which we are all familiar: the decrees, the expulsions, the *hurban*. In the Bible, Pharaoh decrees the murder of every Jewish male baby (Ex. 15–22). The Bible's case of infanticide feels so grotesque and abhorrent to Jewish culture. It has been a repeated theme throughout our many genocidal experiences.

Ultimately, in the sixth and final stage—the aftermath— the sweeping antisemitic destructive explosion forces the Jewish experience to end in Egypt. A force arrives to bring salvation, and we collectively survive. In the biblical case, God redeems the Jewish people through the leadership of Moses and frees us from the bondage of Egypt (Ex. 2–12). We leave that diaspora, anxiously trying to find a new society in which to live.

Every diaspora endures these six cycles: entrance, adaptation, success, new treatment, explosion, and aftermath. Egypt welcomed Joseph's brothers and then enslaved their descendants. Spain was welcoming and forward-thinking before its inquisition and expulsion. Germany was enlightened and rational before the Final Solution.

The United States has proven warm and hospitable to Jews for a long time. This country has afforded us unparalleled opportunity. Then, the college campus protests arrived, and encampments spread rapidly across this country. While it's not fully clear whether we are still in the phase of success in America (stage 3) or have begun the stage of new treatment (stage 4)—the tremors, it seems, have begun.

Too many people around me speak of America as if *this* is the final explosion. It is not. In the 2024 presidential elections, we had two candidates who each argued that they were friends to American Jews and to Israel. Poll after poll reveal that an overwhelming majority of Americans stand by the Jewish population and support the State of Israel. Can American Jews behave differently from every other diaspora group of Jews as it progressed through the stages?

I believe we can, because America is different. As American Jews, we are endowed with the same blessings of freedom and liberty as all other Americans. It's not too late. We're not close to the end of the cycle. I know this truth, because my family has already lived through the sixth stage.

~

I am the product of righteous people. Rabbi Moshe Feinstein famously described all survivors of the Shoah as righteous. Having never met my grandparents, he described them impeccably. All four of them were born in Eastern Europe, survived the raging genocidal inferno that was the Shoah, and then decided to immigrate to the United States of America. They all arrived in Chicago and profoundly believed that America offered a vastly different experience for Jews than Europe had.

Many reading this book may say, dismissively, that America today looks nothing like Germany in 1939. Thank God it doesn't. I know from my family's experience that if our streets looked like Germany in 1939, then we'd be too late. America today does not resemble any of the places in which we experienced final calamities: Iran in 1979, Morocco in 1955, Iraq in 1951, Spain in 1492, England in 1290. The list could go on and on.

On the day Jewish life in each of those places ended, they did not precisely mirror one another either. Yet the pattern they share is clear.

Another example: The expulsion of Jews from Spain in 1492 was the final earthquake explosion after years of tremors. Only one hundred years earlier in 1391, the Jewish community of Spain experienced a massacre: A raging pogrom of murder and plunder engulfed the country, as four thousand Spanish Jews were murdered. Upon their expulsion from Spain 101 years later, I'm sure the grandchildren of those families left their homes in disbelief. I am confident that they boarded ships and crouched onto wagons, thinking, "How could this have possibly happened in Spain?"

It's easy to ignore each tremor as minor. It's convenient to explain away each spike of antisemitism as an aberration. It's easy to believe the outburst will subside. On the other hand, it's challenging to recognize the truth. The truth lies in the tremors. They reveal a trajectory toward catastrophe.

Right now, we are living through a dramatic surge in antisemitism in the United States and around the world. Some of America's youngest generation of leaders are embracing anarchy, fanaticism, terrorism, and Jew-hatred as virtues in this moment of moral inversion. I would be remiss not to acknowledge the trend as a Jewish leader today. I would be culpable if I did not help facilitate new ideas to buck this trend. We must learn from the past and not allow history to repeat itself.

—

To understand the truth of our current tremors, we must explore the anxiety and anguish of our recent past here in the United States. The diaspora today extends beyond the United States, but not by much. Today, approximately 90 percent of global Jewry lives in America or Israel. To simplify, let's say that approximately 45 percent of Jews live in the United States. According to the Jewish Agency data from 2022, the next three largest communities in the diaspora—French, Canadian, and British Jews—together count for less than 8 percent of the global Jewish population. And their populations are decreasing. The future of the diaspora is bound to the future of America's Jews.

The circumstance of diaspora Jewry is now a reflection of the circumstance of Jewish life in America. The last couple of decades of Jewish life in America can be categorized with one word: tumultuous.

To my mind, President Barack Obama's inauguration in 2009 ushered in an atmosphere of acute divisiveness within the American Jewish community. While he certainly surrounded himself with many Jewish advisors, they treated Israel differently than did previous Democratic administrations. Obama admitted that treating Israel with a greater even-handedness would be better for America within the global community. While he convinced a great number of Jews and others to trust in his strategy, any distancing from Israel also signaled a moral obfuscation in our global leadership as well.

This Obama-era shift began to separate American Jews in two key ways. First, Obama meddled within the organizational structure of the Jewish community, elevating Jewish organizations previously considered marginal. The clearest example of this was J Street. On September 9, 2009, *The New York Times* published an article by James Traub called "The New Israel Lobby," which documented the meteoric rise of J Street and its leader, Jeremy Ben-Ami, fueled by the Obama administration. The agenda of this new "Israel lobby" was to distance American Israel policy away from the wishes of Israel.

In April 2010, President of Israel Shimon Peres welcomed J Street, which served its agenda as a pro-Israel lobby. Since that meeting, Israeli governments—liberal and conservative alike—have largely distanced themselves from J Street. J Street's elevation has paved the way for other, far more threatening organizations, such as IfNotNow in 2014. None of these organizations affect policy in Israel. Thus far, their great accomplishment is the nurturing of contention and fracture within the American Jewish community.

The second way in which the Obama administration wrought havoc on the American Jewish community was through the policy of engaging with the Islamic Republic of Iran. The American recruitment of the United Kingdom, France, Germany, Russia, and China into the negotiation with Iran prompted a dramatic shift toward the normalization of a fundamentalist, terror-supporting, theocratic regime. This perspective argued that Americans should welcome Iran's pro-terror Jew-hatred back into the community of nations. In a 2014 interview on NPR, Obama said that Iran could become a "very successful regional power" once it was "reintegrated into the international community."

Obama's Iran policy caused a great chasm within the American Jewish community. We were forced to side with the worldview of President Obama and the Iran Deal or side with Prime Minister Benjamin Netanyahu and his perspective that attempted to prevent the world from negotiating with Iran. This all culminated in Netanyahu's direct address to a joint session of Congress on March 3, 2015. Some American Jews welcomed Netanyahu as the global Jewish leader, while others viewed his speech as inappropriate and threatening to our calm, successful diasporic existence.

In one of his last acts as president, Obama's two terms ended with a final slap at Israel. In December 2016, he, Secretary of State John Kerry, and UN Ambassador Samantha Power officially abstained and unofficially aided the passing of UN Security Council Resolution 2334. Lauded by the Palestinian Authority as a great victory, Resolution 2334 demands the cessation of all Israeli building in eastern Jerusalem and the territories. Israeli representatives described a feeling of abandonment. The resolution stepped beyond previous international demands—eastern Jerusalem includes the Old City, the site of the Western Wall, viewed by Jews worldwide as an inviolable part of the eternal spiritual and political capital of the Jewish people.

While President Obama's election offered hope to so many minorities, Jews clearly fell outside the intersectional minority coalition. This did not bother many American Jews; indeed, he left office popular among our community. He had tried to address many social injustices within American society and was celebrated for it. One of the intended consequences of his worldview was that by empowering minority groups, he fostered alliances between previously unassociated minorities such as African Americans and Arab Americans. These alliances would give rise to a new concept of "diversity, equity, inclusion," or DEI, that would sweep across the educational and business sectors. DEI, however, almost inevitably brands Israel as a colonialist power and holds all Jews accountable as an extension of the structural oppression caused by whites instead of celebrating Israel as a model of an indigenous people flourishing in their ancestral homeland and Jews as a minority that overcame discrimination and found success.

Then, President Donald Trump oversaw a bipolar period for the American Jewish experience. Following his victorious, polarizing campaign, filled with apologetics for known racists and acceptance of support from extremists, on August 12, 2017, the Unite the Right Rally welcomed white nationalists, Klansmen, and neo-Nazis of every stripe to Charlottesville,

Virginia. That evening, evil was illuminated for the world by tiki torches as a bloodthirsty crowd of antisemites in khaki marched, chanting, "Jews will not replace us." The American Jewish community watched in horror as the ghosts of Nazis past found new life in America. Not since the Nazi march in Skokie, Illinois, in 1979 was there such a public gathering of Nazis meant to intimidate American Jews. Trump's relationship with the majority of the American Jewish community was so fraught that his condemnation of antisemitism was largely overshadowed by the barrage of his bewildering news cycles.

A year later, on October 27, 2018, an anti-immigrant white supremacist walked into the Tree of Life Synagogue in Pittsburgh and murdered eleven worshippers and wounded six during a Shabbat service. The victims included Shoah survivors and Jews with special needs. On April 27, 2019, during Passover services, a white supremacist carrying an AR-15 rifle entered a Chabad house in Poway, California. He killed one worshiper and injured three others, including the rabbi. I grew up in an America in which synagogues did not require secured entry, teams of armed guards, and panic buttons that we now have in many synagogues around the country. One can walk into a church or a mosque in America without concern or security, but the Jewish community now needs guards and arsenals to gather and pray in peace.

And yet, Trump also made decisive moves in support of Israel. On December 6, 2017, the United States of America officially recognized Jerusalem as the capital city of the State of Israel. Trump delivered on a campaign promise made by every presidential candidate, Democrat and Republican, for decades since it was first demanded by congressional legislation in 1995: He officially recognized Jerusalem as the capital of the State of Israel.

This momentous decision, however, was met with a deafening silence by the American Jewish community. Most American Jews, proudly Democratic and unwilling to grant Trump any kind of "win," refused to celebrate the occasion. It was a tragic lost opportunity for the American Jewish community. It was a lost opportunity for us to express our joy, our gratitude, and our pride in our Zionism. By that point, we had been sufficiently confused and bewildered by the barrage of Trump's erratic behavior that we couldn't celebrate the formal recognition of our longed-for ancient capital.

Shortly thereafter, the tremendous international accomplishment of the Abraham Accords—a new peace initiative between Israel and several Gulf states—met with Jewish confusion concerning Trump fueled by the divide between a Jewish community that supported these decisions for Israel's sake and those American Jews who stood opposed to Trump no matter the topic. The Abraham Accords should have inspired our community with a new sense of possibility and optimism for a new Middle East that accepts Israel as a neighbor and partner. But living on a seesaw is not easy or comfortable.

There is no doubt that President Trump's campaigns allowed for the normalization of right-wing white nationalism and antisemitism in American society in a way that had never before been accepted. He championed a revolting coalition of malcontents that fed off of a racist other-blaming trope that permeated our national conversation for four years. Americans fought and died to defeat Nazism. Any sympathy shown toward white nationalists—Nazis—is a betrayal of American values and an insult to the good Americans who fought and died in Europe during World War II.

Trump left the White House claiming to have been the best American president for Israel in history—as had Obama, who, alongside his dealings with Iran, had also passed an unprecedented $10 billion package of military aid to Israel. What the two had in common was this: They both behaved in ways that compelled most American Jews to separate their support for Israel from their Jewish identity. We were trapped in a choiceless choice.

President Biden was elected on a platform of calm adulthood and steady judgment. After four years of rocky news cycles, Biden promised to restore dignity to the Oval Office. Then, Russia invaded Ukraine in 2022. The United States adopted a policy to help Ukraine resist Russian incursion, but we keep refusing to give Ukraine the necessary support to win the war.

Then, October 7 happened. Along with Jews everywhere, I felt so proud to see President Biden stand shoulder-to-shoulder with Israel. American aircraft carriers moved into the Mediterranean and aided in Israel's defense. On April 13, the United States Armed Forces aided in Israel's defense from an onslaught of hundreds of Iranian drones and missiles.

At the same time, President Biden's administration tried to appease Israel's critics and kowtowed to the progressive, pro-Palestinian wing of his party. For example, on March 7, 2024, Biden utilized exaggerated statistics provided by the

Hamas Ministry of Health during his State of the Union Address. Those cited statistics validated the false claims of the pro-Palestinian camp on the global stage. Members of his administration have called for a new government in Israel and even participated and fueled the global charade of investigating Israel for committing war crimes. For many months, he placated progressives and played with matches until, one day, the whole box caught fire.

On April 17, 2024—only several days after Iran bombarded Israel with over three hundred rockets—students at Columbia University and outside organizers staged a "Gaza Solidarity Encampment" in the center of the Manhattan campus. They chose the same day as Columbia President Nemat Shafik was questioned by Congress for her inability to curb antisemitism. For weeks, the encampment grew in strength, expressed more contempt for Jews and vitriolic hatred for Israel, and spread across college campuses throughout the country. For weeks, college administrators tried negotiating with the pro-Hamas students.

On April 21, a rabbi who works on the campus urged Jewish students to leave for their own safety. On April 23, Columbia accommodated the Jewish students who felt uncomfortable on campus and threatened by the protests by changing their courses to hybrid learning, affording the Jew-hatred a victory. Then, on May 1, the New York Police Department raided the campus and arrested hundreds in an attempt to restore order. However, campus encampments at UCLA, Berkeley, and Northwestern powered on. University presidents dithered, threatening punishments, but eventually retracted their positions.

Whether dealing with terrorists based in Gaza or their supporters burrowing on American campuses, we must battle them, so they do not inflict their corrosive worldview on our way of life. We must not compromise our ideals.

Israel must remain a core element of our modern Jewish identity. Any political figure that begins to separate Jews from Israel is destructive. Any political figure that offers sanctuary to those who seek to harm Jews is reckless.

The problem transcends the tedious left-right divisions of the moment. Only one member of Congress flies a foreign flag outside her office, and that is a Palestinian flag outside the office of Democratic Representative Rashida Tlaib. Tlaib's vitriolic Jew-hatred epitomizes liberal antisemitism. Republican Representative Marjorie Taylor Greene represents the ignorant conservative fringe conspiracy theorists after her accusation of Rothschild-funded "space solar generators" that ignite wildfires in California, which became known as the "Jewish space lasers" claim. Sixteen years of Obama, Trump, and Biden have wedged the American Jewish community into an unpopular middle in a political system in which nobody caters to the moderate middle any longer. Each successive primary season introduces more extreme characters and challenges us to consider greater compromise for our future as Jews in America.

Since the Hamas attack on Israel on October 7 and Israel's obligation to fight a rightful, just war, the American Jewish community now sits between two loud, dark forces on the United States political fringes that intend to intimidate and to harm us. In many ways, these two fringe movements from opposite sides of the political spectrum have now aligned in agreement. The far left and the far right do not agree on economics, foreign policy, education, immigration, or social welfare. They agree only on Jew-hatred.

~

My grandparents lived through the most iconic phase of explosive, catastrophic Jew-hatred during the Shoah. While I could retell the stories of all of my grandparents—whom I lovingly called Ba and Gammi and Papa Nathan and Gramma Fay—in this instance, I will focus on one of them. The aftermath of October 7 here in America has forced me to reflect on their decisions openly and honestly for my own sake and the sake of our collective family, our collective people.

Papa Nathan—for whom I am named—survived concentration camps and was liberated by the light of liberty of the American military. He returned to Poland to see if his family had survived. It was there that he learned that his wife and daughter from before the war had been murdered in a concentration camp. So, he mustered the strength to begin again. After the end of the Shoah, while in hiding from the local Poles and Soviet soldiers, who all detested the Jews for surviving and continued attacking Jewish men and sexually assaulting Jewish women after the war, Papa managed to meet and marry my Gramma.

Four Jewish men held the four corners of a *tallit*, and they stood together under a *huppah*—a Jewish wedding canopy— and married in a custom that dates back thousands of years.

44

They returned to our tradition and found strength and comfort in the customs of our people. From there, they moved to a Displaced Persons camp in Germany so that they could have a better chance of immigrating to join his family in America.

In that DP Camp, Papa and Gramma began a new family with the birth of my aunt. That birth and a subsequent illness caused them to miss their first two ships to America. Then, Papa's daughter from before the war, Luba, arrived to the DP Camp and finally found her father. In that shocking moment, Papa discovered that Luba was in fact alive. Now an older teenager, Luba explained that she saw her mother, Papa's first wife, beaten to death at Auschwitz. Miraculously, Luba survived.

Papa and Gramma immediately invited Luba to join them on their voyage to America. Luba declined and explained that her future resided with the other teens who were set to fight for a Jewish state in our ancestral homeland. Papa and Gramma had no interest in fighting anymore. They had been sufficiently wounded: more than two hundred members of my family were murdered across Europe. Papa helped Luba reach her ship to Israel and helped Gramma and his new family board their ship to America. In that decision to come to America, Papa and Gramma decided once again to place their faith in life in the diaspora.

Diaspora is defined as our Jewish existence outside of the Land of Israel. Since antiquity, Jews have stood divided in our manner of commitment to our ancestral inheritance that is the Land of Israel. Many of us consider ourselves committed to Israel from the diaspora. The diaspora affords us economic opportunities to support our peoplehood and our statehood from afar. The diaspora offers us the opportunity to rally support for Israel among our neighbors and our governments. The diaspora lends us the freedom to visit Israel countless times and enjoy the culture, the cuisine, and the connection. Many of us think this is the best we can do given the circumstances of our lives. After all, we were born *here*, and it would be challenging to uproot our lives and move *there*.

It does not have to be this way. The assumptions of the six-stage cycle of diaspora and our current relationship with Israel should not be accepted without consideration. Our lives reflect our choices. Often, as Jews, we choose diaspora. We continue to choose diaspora today.

The Book of Ezra recounts that when offered the opportunity to leave Babylonia and return to the Land of Israel, many Jews decided not to return and to remain in exile in Babylonia. In just over a century, the Babylonian Jewish community had grown accustomed to life in Babylonia. Archaeology proves that a Jewish diaspora in Alexandria, Egypt, developed even before the destruction of the Second Temple in Jerusalem. There is a segment of our people that has always preferred to live under the thinly veiled experience of peace and prosperity among our neighbors. That is, until the veil tears.

Diaspora is a thinly veiled experience. It can appear that Jews are safe, but that façade can disappear quickly. Its serenity and surplus can cover its dangers for only so long. When the veil tears, the ugliness of antisemitism pierces through and envelopes the Jewish world.

Rabbi David Hartman famously discussed the theme of the "thinly veiled" existence concerning the High Holiday liturgy. The holiday prayers point out the fragility of life because they aim to shatter complacency. Our comfort is not the primary focus of Judaism. Our Jewish existence is meant to push us away from comfort and toward meaning. When the thin veil of diaspora fractures, then choices we have made in favor of economic wealth, familiarity with language and culture, and surrounding family are all called into question. It feels like the outburst of Jew-hatred has torn the veil and forced us to reconsider our choices.

Today's American diaspora has once again approached a moment of crisis. Can the Jewish people live our fullest identity within our current diaspora? Are we destined to live and relive the biblical diasporic cycle again?

My grandparents lived through the six cycles and chose to return to the comfort of the thin veil of diaspora. I want my children to see the unvarnished truth of our existence. I want them to recognize the profound sense of decency and morality that most Americans share. I want them to be sensitive to feel the tremors of the loud anarchist, pro-terror cowards who sully our streets. I want them to choose paths forward that feel the tremors and acknowledge the truth.

I want my children to live without any veil over their eyes. Jews have to retain their senses.

In order to prevent our past from becoming our present, we have to understand our recent history and our place within the biblical cycles of diaspora. We must make choices that forge a different path forward for our people. All emergencies scare those who are uninformed and unprepared. We must approach the current tremors with a degree of thoughtfulness and planning. Just because I don't believe that we are near the end of our sequence of diasporic phases is not a reason to ignore the warning signs and begin preparation. For us, the most significant preparation is required within.

CHAPTER 2

The Problem of Dual Loyalty

The provocative nature of this book's title reveals a condition of Jewish experience in the diaspora. There should not be anything scary about the title, but every Jewish reader of early drafts cautioned me about breaking a taboo. Social norms are exploding all around us. Let's begin to consider why we feel so uncomfortable with the straightforward expression of American Jewish dual loyalty to the United States of America and the State of Israel.

Thousands of years of persecution and emigration have encouraged Jews to value adaptation and assimilation. Generations of diasporic Jews have desired acceptance into a host culture. Our people's compass has pointed outward toward becoming authentically other. We must recalibrate the compass to point inward toward our own sense of peoplehood.

While America is genuinely different in character than every other diaspora, we cannot consider our current situation in a vacuum. We must begin by reflecting on the history of choices that have led us to this point. This is not the first significant opportunity in which we have tried to calculate a different path forward. We will look at the last historical turning point that set us on this modern path, then explore a long repeating history of Jew-hatred that forced Jewish migration across Europe, and, finally, the unique American challenge—historically and personally.

—

In my modern European history course for my PhD at Claremont Graduate University, the French Revolution served as the starting point. It is impossible to select any single moment or event to mark such a transition between the Middle Ages and modernity. Certainly, nobody living in Europe awoke in May 1789 and witnessed the convening of the Estates General and consciously understood that they now lived in modernity. Nevertheless, the French Revolution's call for liberty, equality, and fraternity stood as a lighthouse for Europeans trying to navigate their way toward new enlightened thought. That new thought process led to the modern concept of citizenship.

The significance of the French Revolution for the purposes of this research isn't solely the promise of liberty for the masses. Part of that new enlightened thought reconsidered the status of Jews as fully emancipated citizens. In many ways, we still feel the reverberations of the decisions made in France throughout the nineteenth century, because they poured a new foundation for social and political enlightened thought that we can still feel today. The truth is always in the tremors.

This turning point must be examined thoroughly for two reasons. First, Europe was home to the majority of world Jewry by the end of the eighteenth century. This is why the promise of the Enlightenment—which included the rise of liberalism, its fusion with nationalism, the appreciation of science, and the Industrial Revolution—proved so disappointing when, almost two centuries later, all of these trends ultimately led to the billowing smoke of death camps across Europe.

Second, up until the French Revolution, Jews never stood to gain equal standing as to our Christian neighbors on such a grand scale. While it's true that the guarantee of the American Revolution that "all men are created equal" included Jews, the Jeffersonian pledge meant nothing to Europe's population where the majority lived. In Europe itself, while previous eras might have included moments of optimism in which Jews were granted more rights, the feudal system of pre-Enlightenment Europe saddled Jews with an inferior status that felt impossible to overcome. The empire-building ambition of Napoleon resulted in a widespread opportunity in which the totality of Europe's Jews might have benefited from the judgment of a single benevolent emperor.

Although the revolution began in 1789, it progressed through different stages until the rise of Napoleon Bonaparte. The nineteenth century for Jews in France began with the hope of Napoleon and ended with the condemnation of Dreyfus. Why did such a dramatic turn of events occur within the nineteenth century? Have we learned the correct lessons from that century of Jewish experience in France?

While the authors of the French Revolution championed liberty, equality, and fraternity, the Jews of France considered whether those same liberal notions of citizenship would be extended to Jews. Napoleon brought great hope to Jewish communities throughout Europe. As his military campaign swept across Europe and the Mediterranean, Napoleon insisted on the emancipation of each territory's Jews as they fell under his control. While emancipation from the limited societal roles of the Middle Ages was a step forward, it was not clear that Jews would fully participate as citizens and enjoy the protection of the new enlightened laws of the modern nation-state.

In 1806, Napoleon summoned an Assembly of Notables of the Jewish Community to meet and discuss with him a myriad of issues concerning the possibility of Jews receiving equal rights throughout Europe. Broadly speaking, he sought to understand better whether Jews could ever be understood as loyal citizens of their respective nation-states—and thus participate in and enjoy the promise of the French Revolution. Napoleon asked: Could Jews ever be understood as true Frenchmen? Can Jews reconcile their *halacha,* or Jewish legal system, with the secular modern French set of laws?

The Jewish community understood the historic possibility embedded within Napoleon's curiosity. One year later, the French Jewish community established for itself an official court to respond, known as the French Sanhedrin. The French Sanhedrin comprised seventy-one Jewish leaders, two-thirds of whom were rabbis and one-third secular leaders. Led by the Chief Rabbi of Strasbourg, David Sinzheim, that Sanhedrin explained the Jewish traditions of holding our law and customs in a subservient position to the law of the state, including our customs of *ketuba* (marriage contract) and *get* (bill of divorce). The French Sanhedrin made the case that Jewish customs were able to fit within the national framework of any foreign state. The body worked tirelessly to allay fears and gain equal stature for Jewish citizens throughout Europe.

Jewish communities across Europe viewed Napoleon as a messianic figure and anticipated his arrival to their nation as a moment of rescue. Not since Moses had one individual arisen for the Jewish people with the promise of widespread emancipation. Liberty stood as the great pledge of the Enlightenment. The thought that Enlightenment principles might be extended to Jews forced all of Europe—Jews and non-Jews—to consider the transformational power of the moment.

According to scholar Simon Schwarzfuchs in his work *Napoleon, the Jews, and the Sanhedrin*, Napoleon issued a worrisome proclamation to the Sanhedrin after its deliberations were well underway. The Sanhedrin accommodated the emperor's wishes on every item except for condoning mixed marriage. In 1806, the French minister of the interior, Jean-Baptiste Champagny, suggested an invitation for all French Jews to take an oath of loyalty to France to obtain citizenship. In 1807, the emperor asked further that the Jewish leaders delineate between religious and political views. For the first time in Jewish history, a foreign leader asked Jews to separate our religious practices from our people's political aspiration to return to Zion. Our acceptance as Frenchmen depended upon our rejection of Zionism. To understand it another way, how could Jews be loyal to France while yearning to return to a promised land elsewhere?

This dilemma for the Sanhedrin epitomizes the longstanding concern for dual loyalty. How can one be a loyal citizen in the diaspora while we face eastward three times each day and pray for a rebuilt Jerusalem? How can people be loyal citizens of a country while they end their Passover Seder with the phrase, "Next year in Jerusalem"?

The Sanhedrin struggled with the question. This stood as a more difficult challenge than whether the rabbis would acknowledge a civil marriage or civil divorce. This new line of questioning strikes at the core of our daily prayers and a central tenet of the Hebrew Bible that Jews will always yearn ultimately to return to the land promised to our ancestors as our inheritance.

The end of the Napoleonic reign brought an end to the glimmer of hope for the Jews of Europe. Less than ten years later, as Napoleon's grip over Europe began to loosen, communities exhibited considerable backlash against their Jewish populations. After a public consideration of Jewish national rights across the different burgeoning European nation-states, they all seemingly agreed that Jews did not deserve equal status.

Franz Kobler ends his book *Napoleon and the Jews* by addressing the aftermath of this Jewish opportunity in history. Kobler concludes, "Napoleon himself, with his lack of understanding of Jewish tradition, seemed a hostile force rather than a patron of the Jewish people." I do not believe that the Sanhedrin failed or in any way carried responsibility for Napoleon's ultimate hostility. They simply fell into the trap of diaspora. Again, diaspora demands a degree of assimilation in order to survive.

The members of the Sanhedrin were themselves conditioned to diasporic expectations. They should have rejected the question of loyalty from the outset. Embedded with the question of loyalty for Jews is a deep-seated accusation. It resembles the leading question, "How long have you been beating your spouse?" For a Jew to answer any question about loyalty is to reinforce the premise of our accusers.

This binary demand for loyalty has always forced us into certain demise. No matter which path we choose or how we answer the question, no diaspora has been able to sustain our tradition for much longer than two centuries. As a result, since the French Revolution, Jewish leadership has encouraged Jews to remain loyal to the modern nation-state with a troubling disregard for the teachings of our own tradition. This lesson is a modern byproduct of Napoleon's gesture.

None of us know Napoleon's true intentions, but his highlighting the question of liberty for Jews forced Europe to face its traditional scapegoat with genuine consideration. This episode also taught Jews an important lesson. Rather than understand Enlightenment ideals as inclusive for them, they would need to apply the Enlightenment principles of nationalism and liberty for themselves in a location outside of Europe. Accordingly, Jewish nationalism arose to focus on the establishment of a Jewish state.

At the same time, Enlightenment thinkers in North America created another experiment in liberty and democracy known as the United States of America. Here, we are all immigrants or the descendants of immigrants, and we are all Americans. There is not supposed to be a litmus test of loyalty. Yet, the provocative nature of the title of this work surely brings unease to American Jews who see it. Why?

We carry with us the experiences of thousands of years of diaspora. As much as we trust in the American dream and all of the blessings this incredible country has afforded its Jewish citizens, we know that we are in the diaspora. Jews continue to fall back into repeated tropes, especially of the nineteenth century. Some American Jews justify this troubling moment and try to keep America's reputation intact. They are Dreyfus. Some American Jews insist that now is the moment to begin formulating our plan to leave. They are Herzl.

Yet, there is another path.

Our peoplehood is rooted in our sacred texts, our religious practices, our language, our cuisine, our music, our cuisine, our dance, and our cuisine. We are a vast tapestry of traditions sewn from different beautiful hues from around the world. Even from America, we are bound to Jewish brothers and sisters around the world. We stand devoted to Israel as well.

Dual loyalty is a notion that our loyalty cannot and should not be contained within national boundaries. Our Jewish tradition and our sense of peoplehood demand more of us. Dual loyalty rejects Napoleon's questions and the French Sanhedrin's mission. Jews should be accepted, not within a French framework, or within an American framework. We should simply be accepted.

The Enlightenment-era conception of nationalism that begins with the French Revolution considering the possibility of Jews as equal citizens, eventually turns back to the scapegoating of Captain Dreyfus in Paris as the ultimate traitor. The disappointment of France's nineteenth-century choices ultimately fuels Herzl's authorship of *The Jewish State* in 1895.

In many ways, Herzl realized that if Jews could not be free in enlightened France, there would ultimately never be a suitable diaspora for the Jewish future. I surmise that he wrote *The Jewish State* aware of the American promise. If I could ask him anything, I would love to find out why he profoundly believed that Europe's Jews should return home to fight for a State of Israel rather than find refuge in the United States. How did he see it so differently than my grandparents?

I would appreciate his insight. And, I would thank him for his life's work.

⁓

My grandparents immigrated to America because they had family who lived here and sponsored them. Yet, their arrival here was not easy, and they faced unnecessary cruelty.

My Papa Nathan and Gramma Fay were treated so poorly by family that they chose to move out with a young toddler daughter. The only apartment they hoped to afford was the basement unit of an old building. Papa Nathan worked outdoors peddling goods on Chicago's famous Maxwell Street market. Gramma Fay also worked to contribute.

Soon after they moved into their own apartment in the basement, they complained to the building's Jewish manager about rats in the basement. The manager smiled at them in a condescending fashion. "Those rats are citizens here," he said. "You are not."

Ba and Gammi moved out of their relative's unit shortly after their arrival as well. Ba was informed that Jews in America don't work as rabbis or cantors. This country attracted Jews because of its religious tolerance. Then, in an effort to transform into authentic Americans, Jews encouraged other Jews to shirk their traditions. They simply couldn't imagine a balance between traditional values and our new American values.

Papa Nathan worked tirelessly his entire life to eke out a living and support his wife and two daughters. After grueling days of work on Maxwell Street, he and Gramma Fay attended night school and learned English and American civics. They proudly passed their citizenship test. A long distance from the traditions of Lodz, he believed that education was key to American success, even for his daughters. Both of his daughters earned college scholarships and degrees.

Papa Nathan died years before I was born. I live as one of his namesakes. During my childhood, Gramma Fay told me the story of her citizenship test hundreds of times. She was so proud of her status as an American citizen. Like so many Americans born here, I grew up largely taking my place here in this country for granted. Papa Nathan and Gramma Fay, and Ba and Gammi, struggled for acceptance in America. Until the end of their lives, they took great pride in their English penmanship and never spoke ill of this country.

At the same time, Papa Nathan refused to let go of fundamental Jewish values in the face of American culture. He and Gramma Fay upheld *kashrut* (Jewish dietary laws), and he wore his *tallis* (prayer shawl) and *tefillin* (phylacteries) every morning. They spoke Yiddish with their friends while they played cards, but they gave their daughters very American names.

With all of the financial and cultural struggles to be American, Papa Nathan never forgot to send money to Israel for Luba. Gramma Fay always understood that their financial hardship here was not an excuse for selfishness. Both of them remembered real scarcity and appreciated the opportunity to live in a land of plenty. During its infancy, Israel was still an economic desert. Papa Nathan tried to provide for Luba as well. In his own way, his life exemplified a life of dual loyalty, although I'm sure he would have feared that phrase.

My grandparents tried to find a balanced life between their Americanism and their Judaism. Their Judaism felt different. They knew more about Judaism than my friends' American grandparents. As a family, we observed more traditions. They took our Jewishness and our peoplehood for granted and sought to add American culture into our homes. At some point between their lives and ours, the balance has been lost. It now needs to be recalculated.

—

Throughout our history, Jews in the diaspora have struggled to find a balance within dominant foreign cultures. Foreign cultures often envelop Jewish communities and challenge the nature of the bond with the larger Jewish people.

Even within the first stage of diasporic experience in Egypt, the text reveals the presence of Jew-hatred. When Joseph has his Egyptian servants serve his brothers food, Genesis informs the reader that, "the Egyptians could not break bread with the Hebrews, since that was an abomination for the Egyptians"

(Genesis 43:32). Rabbi Jonathan Sacks famously referred to that example as the first recorded instance of antisemitism.

More than a thousand years later, Antiochus IV Epiphanes of the Assyrian Greeks attempted to quell Jewish practice. Many Jews in the Land of Israel willingly Hellenized their clothes and names and education and were open to further compromise for the sake of acceptance. Then, in 167 BCE, a priestly family from Modi'in, called the Maccabees, began an uprising to save the tradition. We now commemorate the courage, conviction, and victory of the Maccabees during the holiday of Hannukah. They absolutely rejected loyalty to a foreign culture, foreign rulers, and foreign deities.

Centuries later, after the Roman military had razed the sacred city of Jerusalem to the ground in 70 CE, Flavius Josephus attempted to glorify the Jewish tradition in the eyes of the Romans with his historical compendium *The Antiquities of the Jews*. There is no clear evidence that in Rome the Romans viewed Judaism in a better light as a result of his efforts. The Roman diaspora still exists as one of the oldest, most insular diasporic communities today. When one spends time there, one comes to appreciate how profoundly Roman the Jewish community feels.

And again, a thousand years after that: Invited into England by William I in 1066, Jews encountered a medieval society beginning to flourish and the emergence of a common law legal system that might provide justice for all. Yet, by the early 1200s, antisemitic tropes, including blood libels, spread through the island. English nobleman Simon de Montfort led an uprising of local violence against the London Jewish community, murdering hundreds of Jews. Finally, in 1290, King Edward I ordered the Jewish Edict of Expulsion. In little more than two centuries, England completed its six-step biblical cycle of diaspora.

Jews would not begin to reappear in England until after the Spanish expulsion and not return openly to England until Oliver Cromwell, almost three centuries later. In the next cycle of Jewish settlement, King George II instated a Jew Law in 1753 that allowed Jews to become citizens without pledging loyalty as Christians. After major political blowback, the law was repealed months later. England has maintained a tenuous relationship with its Jewish community ever since, largely dependent on its leadership.

Then, the Pale of Settlement exemplified the biblical six-step cycle of diaspora once again. Toward the end of the eighteenth century, Jews began to look to Eastern Europe toward an area commonly known as the Pale of Settlement. What began as territory controlled by Czarist Russia eventually became Poland, Ukraine, Lithuania, and other nations. Jewish movement was regulated, but new economic opportunities were permitted, such as farming. In the second step, Jewish life flourished in Eastern Europe. In the third step, in response to the success of local Jewish communities, they endured an embryonic stage of Jew-hatred. The hatred manifested into sadistic pogroms that appeared as sudden bursts of violence by the Chmelnitzki and the Haidamacks gangs of thugs in the seventeenth and eighteenth centuries against local Jewish populations in Eastern Europe.

In the fourth step, those violent pogroms eventually spread as more sinister and deadly uprisings condoned by local authorities against their local Jewish populations, such as in Kirovograd and Warsaw in 1881, in Moscow in 1891, in Rostov and Yekaterinoslav in 1883, in Nizhni Novgorod in 1884, in Moscow in 1891, in Kishinev in 1903, in Poland in 1918, and in Romania in 1921, just to highlight a selection of the most brutal. By the time the pogroms reached the horror and scale of the Kishinev Massacre, it was clear that they were intended to destroy the Jewish population.

This marks the arrival of the fifth stage. In the Kishinev Massacre, the local population murdered forty-nine Jews and injured hundreds, looted and destroyed hundreds of homes and hundreds of businesses, and rendered approximately two thousand Jewish families homeless. Russian authorities did not respond to inquiries.

In the sixth stage, the Soviets imprisoned Jews and suppressed Judaism. American Jews led the world in applying pressure for the release of Soviet Jewry. There was a sign to free the Soviet Jewry in front of my childhood synagogue in the suburbs of Chicago. This lasted through the 1980s with the iconic release of the most famous refusenik, Natan Sharansky, in 1986.

The consistency and authority with which these pogroms appeared should lead us to wonder about the toxic conditions of an existence that might allow a group of thoughtful people to accept such a life of fear and unpredictability for centuries. It is easy for us to cast judgment on Jews from these locations as foolish or unworldly.

Yet, I'm not sure how much we've changed. It is perplexing how often I find myself watching the musical *Fiddler on the Roof* in an audience and enjoying the show, when I'm caught off-guard during the innocent, cleaned-up pogrom scene. I find it unnerving and tense, no matter how many times I watch it. Then, the scene ends, and the musical continues, and we return to singing along. Are we all that different from our Eastern European ancestors? Have we really changed our toxic diasporic condition if we so easily redirect ourselves away from pogrom toward singing and choreography?

It is impossible to write a section such as this without acknowledging the Shoah. By reading Amos Elon's portrait of the first three stages of the diaspora German Jewish experience in *The Pity of It All: A Portrait of the German-Jewish Epoch, 1743–1933*, the reader can see that Jews have previously believed that they found true acceptance before the American late-twentieth century. Jews in Berlin felt so thoroughly accepted as Germans that intermarriage rates soared by the early part of the century.

The thin veil of acceptance was fractured on November 9, 1938, by a massive German pogrom known as *Kristallnacht*, otherwise known in English as the "Night of Broken Glass." Over two days in Germany and Austria, 30,000 Jewish men were imprisoned, 7,000 Jewish businesses were devastated, and 267 synagogues were destroyed. Kristallnacht marked the fourth stage of diaspora for German Jews. The fifth stage would give rise to laws that deprived Jews of all rights, businesses, and property—especially as Germany began invading its neighbors to the east in 1939. Jews across Eastern Europe were forced to live in crowded ghettos. My Gramma Fay and Papa Nathan, who lived in Poland, suffered through the depravity of the Lodz Ghetto.

In January 1942, the Wannsee Conference initiated the sixth stage with the conception of the Final Solution, intended to murder every last Jew in Europe and beyond. The Shoah saw Europe systematically mass-murder six million of its Jews—men, women, and children. Approximately one and a half million Jewish children were murdered.

While the inferno of Europe raged, and Jewish bodies billowed into the sky and covered the Earth as ash, the Arab world joined in the process of Jewish extermination. In 1941, the *Farhud*, meaning an explosion of violence in Arabic, occurred across Iraq. Over the course of two days of extreme violence in Baghdad and Basra, more than 150 Jews were murdered, hundreds injured, with reports of Jewish women raped and babies murdered. The explanation given for the *Farhud* was Jewish collaboration with British authorities.

Acceptance and loyalty in the diaspora have always been a challenge for Jews. As much as we aspire toward complete acceptance, no matter whether we try to explain ourselves in French, Russian, German, or Arabic, we are always Jews. There is no sense in trying to hide it any longer.

~

Shlomo M. Brody wrote a fascinating book, *Ethics of Our Fighters*, in which he traces the evolution of Jewish and rabbinic perspectives toward war and the role of soldiers. While rabbinic thought can be traced back for two thousand years, the crux of the research begins during our century of focus in this chapter, the nineteenth century. It only makes sense that during the rise of European nationalism, which coincided with the possibility of European Jewish emancipation, some Jews would ponder their role in defending their nation while others considered whether they should submit to forced military conscription. After all, there is no greater expression of devotion to any cause than one worth giving one's life. Military service expresses nationalism in a deeply profound manner.

Accordingly, Brody references rabbinic rulings that followed the French Revolution and that addressed the forced conscription of Czarist Russia. One of the most significant is that of the influential Rabbi Samson Raphael Hirsch of Frankfurt. Hirsch epitomizes a synthesis of enlightened modernism and traditional Judaism, as he is considered the father of what is known today in America as Modern Orthodoxy. Hirsch argues in favor of the merits of being loyal to one's state to achieve its aims, even if it means sacrificing one's life in service. There can be no greater example of proven loyalty to a nation than a people's willingness to sacrifice its children's lives for its military defense.

This argument by Rabbi Hirsch can be derived from a long tradition of diaspora rabbinic reason that originates in the Talmud. Espoused by the sage Samuel in multiple tractates of the Talmud, the principle is called *dina d'malchuta dina*, Aramaic for "the law of the land is the law." It teaches that when Jewish law concerning civil matters and the law of a foreign state conflict with one another, the rabbinic position is to defer to the state law. Hirsch believed there to be honor in a legally enforced military conscription.

The conception of rabbinic literature following the destruction of the Holy Temple in Jerusalem represents a great moment of Jewish imagination. It took tremendous innovation to imagine a Jewish tradition in which text study and teachers would replace a central temple and priestly responsibilities. Invariably, imagination must be involved whenever the Jewish people take an evolutionary step forward.

We must acknowledge that the same philosophy that has allowed us to flee and adapt and thrive in multiple diaspora settings has also weakened our collective sense of peoplehood. Over the centuries, this prioritization of state law has allowed Jewish communities in Spain, England, Iraq, Poland, Germany, Iran, and America to misunderstand themselves as different from other Jewish communities. In order to survive in different environments, Jews followed the rabbinic doctrine to prioritize the national differences over our bonds of peoplehood.

I am not trying to unravel a two-thousand-year-old rabbinic principle. However, we must understand that Jews were forced to make compromises and adopt them into our diaspora DNA. Jews must now comprehend the ramifications of those policies. To refuse to reconsider the ramifications feels like a failure of imagination. Like the experience of the French Sanhedrin, there is no compromise for any secular European Jew that will ever serve as compromise enough to prove worthy of acceptance.

The United States of America provided new opportunity and new challenges for its Jews. Haym Salomon and other Jews famously played a role in the American Revolution. President George Washington visited the Touro Synagogue in Newport, Rhode Island. The congregation's leadership wrote him a letter of gratitude. Then, in 1790, Washington responded with a letter that proclaimed, "May the children of the stock of Abraham who dwell in this land continue to merit and enjoy the good will of the other inhabitants—while everyone shall sit in safety under his own vine and fig tree and there shall be none to make him afraid. May the father of all mercies scatter light, and not darkness, upon our paths, and make us all in our several vocations useful here, and in His own due time and way everlastingly happy."

The Founding Fathers of this nation extended a different kind of promise of religious tolerance to its Jewish citizens than their European counterparts. The American dream holds out a promise of a future no matter one's past. To look at our American Declaration of Independence as an example, the document acknowledges unalienable rights that include, "life, liberty and the pursuit of happiness." The American Constitution similarly begins with the statement, "We the People of the United States, in order to form a more perfect union...." These ideas set forth a pursuit, a process, a continual perfecting, a dynamic promise for a better future. Jews had never encountered a diaspora with a future promise without prejudice concerning our past. America was established as a different diaspora altogether, truly exceptional.

The concerns about dual loyalty among American Jewry date back well before the establishment of Israel. In 1885—just three years after Leon Pinsker wrote the seminal Zionist text *Auto-Emancipation* and a decade before Herzl wrote *The Jewish State*—the Reform movement felt a need to distance itself from the entire history of Jewish national particularism. "We consider ourselves no longer a nation," the Pittsburgh Platform declared, "but a religious community, and therefore expect neither a return to Palestine, nor a sacrificial worship under the sons of Aaron, nor the restoration of any of the laws concerning the Jewish state."

With the establishment of Israel in 1948, the worry about dual loyalty became more acute. As Daniel Gordis recounts in his book, *Israel: A Concise History of a Nation Reborn*, that same year the president of the American Jewish Committee, Jacob Blaustein, wrote, "We have truly become Americans, just as have all other oppressed groups that have ever come to these shores. We repudiate vigorously the suggestion that American Jews are in exile. The future of American Jewry, of our children and our children's children, is entirely linked with the future of America. We have no alternative; and we want no alternative." The statement embodies arrogance and a failure of imagination. With all of his success and influence in this country, Blaustein was more fearful of what he might lose than what our people might collectively gain.

Ultimately, Blaustein and Ben Gurion would reach a deal that Israel would not actively pursue the immigration of American Jews to Israel. That agreement did not benefit American Jews or Israeli Jews. It foolishly reinforced the notion that the identity on one's passport takes a greater priority over the identity of one's soul. It wrongly portrays a choice between two poles of Jewish life in America and Israel. The agreement sought to address a problem that did not yet exist in American public life.

Blaustein's preemptive pushback against Ben-Gurion and the infant Jewish State is a learned behavior based on life in diaspora. The establishment of the State of Israel might have ended exile, but it did not succeed in eliminating the diaspora. I believe that many American Jews might mistakenly still believe that America is not exile or diaspora, or at least not the same type as the diasporas beforehand. Like Blaustein, they are wrong.

Although American Jewish support for Israel today is strong, the tremors can still be felt from Blaustein's sentiments. Perhaps he did not appreciate the magnitude of the accomplishment of the founding of the State of Israel. Or perhaps, Blaustein understood the promise of the moment in 1948, and also realized how quickly the promise of Napoleon transitions into the demise of Dreyfus.

Dreyfus is the nightmare of every successful diaspora Jew. Deep down, that was Blaustein's fear. Does it still remain a fear of every successful Jew in America? More than seventy-five years later, the adjustment needed for American Jews isn't a recognition of our differences with Israeli Jews, but an admission of our family ties and our shared destiny.

In the conversation about the essential focus of people-hood, the only case scarier for American Jews than Dreyfus is Jonathan Pollard.

⁓

For American Jews, Jonathan Pollard represents a dangerous level of fanatical loyalty to Israel over America. He worked as an American defense analyst, and in 1987, he pleaded guilty to charges of providing classified information to Israel. He was sentenced to life imprisonment. For American Jews, he remains the poster child for the case against dual loyalty. To be clear, the argument in this book is not trying to inspire a generation of Jonathan Pollards. I do not see Jonathan Pollard as proof of dual loyalty. He displayed criminal singular loyalty to Israel.

Pollard committed the crime of espionage and deserved punishment. There are American Jews who must profession-ally weigh their allegiance to the United States of America before any relationship with the State of Israel. Many American Jews serve in the US Armed Forces, the federal government, and even the White House. They must prior-itize their Americanism, certainly in their professional con-text. At the same time, all American Jews should remain con-nected to our sense of Jewish peoplehood, drawing on our collective moral compass that helped navigate a path for the American founders.

In a piece published in *Tablet Magazine* in 2010 titled "National Insecurity: The Case for Jonathan Pollard," Gil

Troy characterized the tension within the American Jewish community concerning Pollard: "Decades into this tragic and pathetic tale, American Jewry's continuing allergy to defending Pollard says more about our communal fears and the price we are willing to pay for social and political acceptance than it does about Pollard and his crimes." Later, Troy noted that with "the terrifying 'dual loyalty' charge—far more terrifying to Jews than to Irish-Americans and other hyphenated Americans—the Pollards defined every Jew's ultimate loyalty as being to the Jewish state."

As Troy repeats again and again, Pollard's guilt must not be confused with his unfairly harsh punishment. For many American Jews, the Pollard case was a litmus test by which we could prove our own Americanism. American Jewish journalists and political pundits stepped forward quickly to condemn Pollard and his dual loyalty. Few American Jews were willing to challenge the judicial system that punished Pollard more harshly than other spies who had committed similar offenses.

I would never advocate for criminal loyalty to Israel that would hurt America. I advocate, rather, for a dual loyalty that acknowledges the special bond between America and Israel, their shared values, and the special role the American Jewish community plays within the relationship. American Jews must strengthen our inner soul to advocate for ourselves and for Jews around the world.

Pollard is a pain point for the American Jewish community on multiple levels. He committed a crime that was intolerable. He suffered a punishment that was demonstrably too harsh. And, when he appealed to the Jewish community for help, too many turned their backs on him. In 2015, Pollard was released from prison.

As a people, we cannot fear dual loyalty because of its most extreme bastardization. To shy away from good ideas because of the rotten apples of the bunch feels like a concession that the entire batch is to be judged according to our worst examples. Pollard does not force us to prove our loyalty any more than Bernie Madoff forces us to prove our fiduciary responsibility. This instinct would paralyze American Jews at every turn in the face of the antisemitism that has risen throughout the United States.

This is a call for Jews to find the strength to bind themselves together, not a call to emulate those whose moral missteps tear us apart.

—

In the nineteenth century, Zionism emerged as an answer for Jews in the diaspora. Without a central idea tethering us all together, we remain fragmented. One would think that Judaism—the tribal practices surrounding the learning of Torah and the practice of mitzvot—would be enough to bond us together. Not so.

Diaspora, with all of its national boundaries, led Jews to mistakenly see themselves as different communities. Antisemitism and all of the challenges of the diaspora drive Jews apart. In the absence of Zionism, the world's Jewish communities lack a singular rallying cry to unite us. In the most recent gathering in Washington, DC, on November 14, 2023, nearly three hundred thousand American Jews (and some allies) convened at the National Mall to protest surging antisemitism and to express support for Israel. The two ideas remain intellectually and practically intertwined.

Israel and the diaspora need one another. Israel anchors the diaspora experience. The diaspora enriches Israel's standing, culture, economy, and defense. Like the double helix model of the DNA, Israel and the diaspora thrive together and shrivel apart.

Why must the two poles be Israel and a diasporic community? Meaning to say, why couldn't two poles develop within the diaspora from which Jews can build relationship and connect? Why didn't Jews in New York feel connected to Jews in Germany in the 1930s? Why didn't Jews around the world reach out and try to save European Jews? Loyalty to diaspora intimidates Jews into a quiet, obedient class. Diaspora encourages Jews to fit into the foreign qualities of the society around us.

In 1896, Theodor Herzl published his political treatise *The Jewish State*. Simply put, he proposed that Jews gather in toward the land of our ancestors and build a utopian society within the Middle East. This new Jewish political entity would serve as the answer to the problems Jews faced in the European diaspora. From the first Zionist Congress in Basel, Switzerland, until 1948, Zionist thinkers convened, considered, and proposed ideas about the creation of a Jewish state.

It is time for the beginning of a new phase of Zionism. We must consider what worked in the past and safeguard those ideas. We must reflect on what concepts failed in the past and bravely discard them. Most of all, we must draw inspiration from the young Israelis, the young soldiers, the young teachers, and young volunteers, who stepped forward and filled the dark void of October 7 to protect a Jewish tomorrow. They had the character and conviction to dare to dream in a moment of nightmare. They inspired me to renew my commitment to this conversation and to propose new ideas for the benefit of us all.

Our young people have once again inspired my optimism for our people. Young Jews have always been able to dream in the face of overwhelming challenges. From the depths of an Egyptian jail, a young dreamer named Joseph emerged. While hiding in a cave, our great Sages studied and taught until they learned it was time to read the morning Shema. While watching our people reduced to a cloud of ashen night, youngsters in the Warsaw Ghetto decided to pick up arms and fight. Opposed by the British and Arab armies in their ancestral homeland, young Jews set out to defend our right to self-determination.

Our ability to dream has always been a Jewish superpower. Dreaming is the only path out of permanent diaspora.

CHAPTER 3

The Jewish Double Helix

Before I reach the argument for the case for dual loyalty, I should acknowledge that I believe that this is an instinct already felt within many American Jews today. We feel it in our hearts. It is time to speak those sentiments of significance aloud. This new priority of peoplehood stems from a primordial Jewish instinct. This pull between two poles has been rooted deep within our souls from the beginning.

The Book of Genesis tells us about our forefather Jacob's journey. In Genesis 28, as he begins his first trek out of the Promised Land to live away from his immediate family and find his extended relatives, he lays his head down to sleep and experiences one of the famous iconic dreams of our tradition. Suddenly, he envisions a ladder that reaches from the ground into the heavens. In the vision, angels ascend and descend up and down the ladder. It is in the context of this ladder dream that God renews his covenant with Jacob.

Colloquially referred to as Jacob's Ladder, this image has been interpreted by Jewish thinkers and artists throughout time. Later given the name Israel, Jacob stands as our collective forefather. The actions of his life, the development of his many children into different tribal elements within our family, and his struggle to keep his family together despite external and internal challenges still inform our identity. After all, more than any other biblical figure, we are still known as his descendants. We maintain the name of the Children of Israel.

That episode has stood as a significant lesson, especially for us, who inherit the dream as a foundational building block for us to understand that we are his children. The dream appears at the precise point at which he is about to experience life outside of the promised land. So, let's return to the ladder to fully appreciate the Bible's vision of life in the diaspora.

The eleventh-century rabbinic sage Rashi brought an interpretation that as Israel left the land—his own land—angels of the land ascended the ladder toward the heavens and diaspora angels descended the ladder toward the earth to protect Israel along his journey through foreign lands. From his home in France, Rashi portrayed a diasporic existence for Jacob that was so significantly foreign to our ancestral promised land that it required a different set of angelic protectors for Israel's sake. Rashi imagines the angels rotating like a line shift in a hockey game.

That is certainly one way to view the ladder. It is easy to focus on the two poles of the ladder and the separation between our promised land and the foreign lands of our diasporic wanderings. This separation represents a zero-sum philosophy in which Israel must choose to exist according to one pole or the other. God and our tradition can travel to any corner of the earth that we choose, but we are either living in the land of Israel or in the lands of diaspora. And, as the angels reveal, there are consequences to the choice.

This conception of Jewish experience has led us to this moment. Israel's journey out of his own land broadly represents the diasporic experience in a condensed form: he flees to find safety in a new diasporic community, he thrives financially and builds a family, and ultimately finds conflict embedded within his own success that forces him to leave. In an ancient world without international borders, Genesis posits that there is only life inside the land or outside the land. Whether it be Haran or Egypt, Europe or America, it is all part of the same category of locations outside of the land, meaning diaspora.

In modernity, Israelis maintain this polarity of thought. They refer to Israelis who live in Israel as living *ba'aretz*, "in the land." They presume that all of diaspora is *hul*, which is a Hebrew acronym that means *hutz la'aretz*, or "outside the land." This division equivocates between the two categories of living inside the State of Israel, roughly 8,500 square miles, and the rest of the world, roughly 57,500,000 square miles. These two options are considered equal without regard to quantity of space or quantity of income (both Abraham and Jacob become wealthy outside the land), because the Bible is concerned about quality of life. The Bible values character and transmitting tradition as the goals of life, not the vast acreage of the outer limits of the world. As Jews, we should still maintain a Genesis worldview in this regard.

Were Jews spread all over the world, perhaps this stark divide might be merited to prevent our destruction within one common home. Yet, that is not the case today. We are not divided throughout the world. We are almost entirely divided between two pronounced locations. This ancient worldview encourages a chasm between the two centers of Jewish life today: Israel and America.

The Jewish people bought into this portrait of a growing rift for the last several decades. Every study portrayed two Jewish communities moving in divergent directions. Israeli and American Jews, it was claimed, were losing understanding for one another, and it was largely believed that they no longer supported one another. Allegedly, we lived according to two separate value systems of two different places. It was previously believed that American Jews valued individual responsibility and universal acceptance, whereas Israeli Jews valued communal responsibility and a particularistic perspective. The aftermath of October 7 shattered that false representation.

Following the horrific tragedy of October 7, American Jews rushed to help, raised money, and rallied its leaders to stand in support of Israel. I arrived in Israel in November and December to find an Israeli society that was devastated and so appreciative of the solidarity. I had never before heard Israelis express gratitude.

Jews share an unbreakable bond that sometimes strains but never severs. Younger generations of Israelis seemingly learned this important lesson in the wake of the October 7 massacre. I believe that younger generations of American Jews learned that the bond of Judaism ties us together more strongly than any other layer of identity. When Israelis are attacked, we feel their pain. When they react, we suffer backlash as well. Jews are always connected with one another.

Instead of the poles, I try to focus on the rungs of the ladder, the infinite bridges that connect the two poles forever. In Genesis, the rungs offer Jacob a path to climb upward, toward his fulfillment. The rungs form the hopeful promise of his ability to ascend the ladder. To focus on the rungs is to choose a Jewish life in relationship with God's promise: the holy land of Israel and the grace of America.

I know many American Jews who have made Aliyah, or moved to Israel, as an expression of their commitment to Israel and our people's narrative. As a child, I believed that those Jews who moved to Israel essentially decided to step onto the stage of Jewish history. American Jews who remained here lived behind the curtain and watched our epic narrative unfold from a distance. I no longer believe that one group is in the spotlight of history and the other remains backstage. There is a more fluid nuance to the way in which Jews live.

October 8 and beyond has revealed to me that the dichotomy is not so stark. Most American Jews live somewhere on the rung. Some of us learned of the barbaric attack, and our instinct was to buy a plane ticket and go help. For those of us, we exist on the rung closer to the Israel pole. Others immediately checked on family and friends there. Many gave money to charitable causes. Some walked into a synagogue for the first time in many years. Few Jews that I know in America didn't at least move slightly closer toward the Israel pole. As the Children of Israel, we all live in relationship with that land and our family which inhabits it. Some of us may feel more comfortable closer to Israel's pole, and others of us may feel more comfortable farther away, but most American Jews live on the rung between the poles of America and Israel.

Previous generations might have watched a deadly pogrom unfold in color videos and run away from our land and our people in search of safety. Catastrophe used to drive Jews away from the rung toward the safety of a foreign diasporic pole. The power and promise of Zionism are the realization that we can only count on ourselves. When danger rears its head, when darkness appears to own the day, we must grasp our own flashlights and work to battle the darkness. After two thousand years of persecution, Zionism preaches to run toward the fire and extinguish it.

Now, the ladder image only presents a two-dimensional representation of our reality. Two dimensions lack the complexity of our world. Our lives more closely resemble a dynamic, shifting reality in which most of us prioritize one or the other at different times depending on current events, personal lifecycles, and national needs. This revolving, spirited ladder more closely forms the shape of our DNA: the double helix.

Rather than two rigid poles that form the ladder, the double helix features two strands that wrap around each other in a constant relationship. As Jews, we orient ourselves around Zion, our ancestral homeland. At the end of the Passover Seder, at the conclusion of telling our people's story, we wish one another, "Next year in Jerusalem." We pray toward Jerusalem from wherever we are in the world. From Los Angeles, I pray facing east. When I visited Dubai, I prayed westward. Israel, in general, and Jerusalem, in particular, form an anchor strand around which our diaspora strand can wind. Our existence anywhere is wrapped around our Jewish existence there.

The Jewish double helix forces us to acknowledge that for American Jews, while the Israel strand wraps around the American strand, the American strand also wraps around the Israel one as well. As a people in diaspora, we continually live out the Jacob's ladder vision of existence.

The rest of the biblical narratives reinforce the vision of the double helix. Before the Babylonians destroyed Jerusalem, we learn that Jeremiah purchased a plot of land to signal our intention to return one day. Why was our eternal connection to our ancestral homeland so important for a people about to face banishment? Centuries later, while remaining in diaspora in Babylonia, Daniel prays out of a window facing toward Jerusalem. Why does the story mention the window? Daniel could not possibly have seen Jerusalem. Would not the text have sufficed to say that he prayed toward the west? What does the detail of the window add?

The window frames the directionality of his soul. The window image implies that, for each of us, there is a notion of a window we can open toward our eternal homeland. *Hatikvah*, the Israeli national anthem, makes this exact claim: "As long as toward the east, to Zion, looks the eye, our hope is not yet lost."

Jews in the diaspora have always lived in relationship with Israel. No matter how far our wanderings veered, we still faced Jerusalem to pray. Whether in English, German, Russian, Arabic, or Farsi—and more often than not simply in Hebrew—we have always concluded our Passover Seder with the declaration, "Next year in Jerusalem." The diaspora strand of the double helix has always revolved around the Israel strand.

This is the power of the ladder image. Whether Jacob chose to climb or descend, it requires him to grasp the rungs. The rungs determine our future. Our Jewish DNA demands strong rungs connecting the two strands. There will always be opposing poles of the DNA structure, and we must focus on strengthening the connecting rungs to allow us to move forward, upward, onward.

How can this new understanding of the ladder image as our collective DNA help inform the Jewish people at this moment?

———

In 1991, my family traveled to Israel for the first time. I was twelve years old. Our rabbi, Rabbi Vernon Kurtz from North Suburban Synagogue Beth El in Highland Park, Illinois, called my parents and told them that he thought they should join the synagogue mission to Israel for first-timers. My parents agreed. In that call, Rabbi Kurtz changed our lives. One cannot underestimate the lasting impact of a good rabbi.

Since that trip, I have visited Israel many, many times. Yet, that first tour brought all of my Zionist instincts to life. Suddenly, Jerusalem was no longer relegated to the pages of the prayer book. It was a real, breathing city. The beach of Tel Aviv came to life. Masada and the Dead Sea—all of it was real. I had never been there before, but at the instant my feet touched the ground, I knew I was home.

During one of the nights of the trip, my family arranged to meet Luba and her family. We met in the lobby of a Tel Aviv hotel. The hotel arranged for a long table, and my family sat on one side, awaiting their arrival. She was a legend in our home. My siblings and I waited curiously, wondering what our family would be like.

We were all raised on Luba's story. She courageously decided to move to British Mandate pre-State Israel with nothing and fight for a Jewish state. She was immediately arrested by the British and imprisoned in Cyprus. There, in another form of a camp, she met and married her husband. Shortly thereafter, they were allowed to take a boat to Israel. As soon as their feet touched the sandy beaches, they were both handed rifles and placed on a bus. That bus drove them down to Yad Mordechai, where it was explained to them that they must hold that line against the oncoming Egyptian army, or Tel Aviv would fall. For my twelve-year-old mind, the story taught me that Luba had saved Israel.

Suddenly, the door opened, and in walked Luba. She looked like nothing I had imagined. She looked short and old and had white hair. There was a round, soft quality to her that resembled my two grandmothers. She looked familiar. She immediately grabbed us and hugged us like we had known each other forever.

Then, her sons walked in with their families. They were tall and strong. They looked like an animator had drawn pumped-up caricatures of our family.

We sat on our side of the table, and they sat on theirs. It was like a family summit. We sat as two delegations.

Luba, her husband, and my parents spoke with one another in English, broken Hebrew, and mostly Yiddish. I sat in silence, staring at my Israeli cousins. We were dressed formally, and they were totally informal. We were silent, and they were carelessly laughing. We were American, and they were Israeli.

Luba asked my parents for me because I was named after her father, Papa Nathan. I looked over and smiled at her. She smiled at me, and then she asked, "Do you want to know how to grow tall and strong like this?"

There was nothing that my twelve-year-old self wanted more.

"Jewish boys end up looking like this in Israel. You have to move to Israel."

At that moment, I wanted to change seats to the other side of the table. I've never stopped wanting to do that.

—

Do Jews move between the strands of the double helix? All the time.

Some Jews have already left the diaspora for Israel. They have made Aliyah and officially affixed themselves to the Israel strand. But many Jews wouldn't leave America even if we were being rounded up in the streets. This is always our reality. Those fringe beliefs are portrayed in the Torah itself.

During the period of our biblical enslavement in Egypt, most readers of Exodus assume it impossible to have escaped from Egypt. Yet, Moses was able to just run away from Egypt and break free into the wilderness (Ex. 2:15). His escape is not described as difficult at all. So, why didn't many other Jews do the same? I'm sure that the journey felt, perhaps even appeared, daunting. And, when it was time for redemption and exodus, an ancient rabbinic tradition tells us that 80 percent of the Israelites decided to remain in the known slavery of Egypt rather than venturing out and pursuing freedom in the unknown. This is human nature. There are American Jews who will not budge from the America strand of the double helix.

My argument is intended for the "middlers." As explained by the Alter Rebbe and the founder of the Chabad movement, Rabbi Shneur Zalman of Liadi, all people within society live their lives on a spectrum. Some live according to the extremes. Yet, most people live within the wide spectrum as middlers. Middlers must be inspired, encouraged, often pushed towards a better path forward. That journey begins with argument and education. The same argument is true for Jews in every respect, including life after October 7.

Most American Jews today—Orthodox, Conservative, Reform, and unaffiliated—live on the rungs between Israel and America. Yes, they believe in a Jewish State of Israel. They believe in American support for Israel. They are not completely in the America strand. Yet, their tolerance for the rising level of Jew-hatred has not forced them to leave. This shows allegiance, trust, and comfort with America despite the anti-Israel protests, pro-terror encampments, and anti-American slogans. There is a significant force that undeniably pulls American Jewry back to the American strand in the double helix. American Jews have to develop the strength and courage to step further out on the rung.

Even with a tremendous sense of faith in America, I encourage my own children to spend more time in Israel. Less and less, I prioritize whether my children attend programs affiliated with a specific denomination of Judaism, and more and more, I prioritize that my children participate in Zionist programming. In an increasingly post-denominational world, American Jews will separate between those solidly affixed to the American pole and those moving on the rung between America and Israel.

The *Jerusalem Post* published an article on May 31, 2024, titled, "American Jews: Over 51% Support Biden's Decision to Withhold Arms from Israel." This research conducted by the Jerusalem Center for Public Affairs reflects an American Jewish community struggling with where it belongs on the rung between America and Israel. Do American Jews trust Israel to conduct the war, or do we trust the president of the United States as a moral and military authority?

This research reflects a constant struggle among American Jews concerning whom to trust and with whom to affiliate. This is nothing new. In 2015, amidst the controversial Obama administration's foreign policy of engaging Iran in nuclear negotiations, Prime Minister Benjamin Netanyahu came to address Congress about the threat of a nuclear Iran and the misguided strategy of the Obama administration. Many American Jews applauded Netanyahu's strong speech, while many others resented his overstep and saw his words as an intentional slap at the president. The American Jewish community reflected the diametrically opposed views of these leaders.

The American Jewish community is not a monolith. We sit as a spectrum between the two strong poles of Jacob's ladder, the revolving double helix. We have always existed on this dynamic range. Following the trauma of October 7 and its aftermath in this country, it is clear that to strengthen our Jewish identity to withstand the next chapter of our diasporic existence, we will need to pull more American Jews into the middle. Our souls will have to draw strength from America and from Israel. Our souls will have to support America and support Israel. American Jews will have to see ourselves as part of this shifting, vital energy bonding together the strands of the DNA.

Herzl conceived of the modern Jewish state as a political solution to the traumas of the diaspora. Three-quarters of a century after its founding, it is clear that Israel's existence does not solve the problems of the diaspora. Israel requires the diaspora, and the diaspora requires Israel. The Jewish people today live within the political, social, and cultural relationship of the double helix between the strand of Israel and the strand of diaspora.

Israel requires support from allies abroad. Those allies—above all, America—are mobilized in large part by Jewish communities around the globe. This diaspora of more than two thousand years forms the other strand of the double helix. Jews have always lived around the world with their minds and hearts pointed to Zion. Jews around the world draw strength from Israel. American Jews should draw strength from Israel. Each side of the double helix nourishes the other.

Yet, too many Jews today still see themselves as fully living on one strand or the other. This false choice is a legacy of the options presented to the Jewish community by Napoleon in the early nineteenth century. Can Jews be French citizens? That Enlightenment logic forced Jews into a corner: In 1806, Jewish leaders in France justified their ability to act as good citizens. It was a mistake.

Even understanding the fundamental differences between America and France, the Enlightenment compelled Jews to justify their ability to conform to citizenship. Understanding their choice, they should have rejected the question. We are still suffering from that same thought process. It is insufficient to live solely on the strand of diaspora.

—

Like most rabbinical students in American seminaries, I spent a year in Israel studying. My wife and our children moved to Jerusalem with me, and we enrolled them in a wonderful preschool.

Approximately one month into our year in Israel, my wife became violently ill. She suffered from stomach attacks that forced her into Hadassah Hospital for five days. She underwent many tests.

While all of the doctors at Hadassah spoke fluent English, the nurses and staff did not. My wife spoke little Hebrew, and certainly not enough to feel comfortable in the hospital.

I spent my time racing between the hospital to be by her side and trying to watch over our kids. We had neighbors, whom we didn't know at all, offer to help watch the kids after school. When I told my parents, they reacted loudly, "Who are these people? Strangers?"

They were strangers. And they also felt like family. How could that be?

Well, many, many families in Israel were built by people who left the comfort and trust of extended family in the diaspora and made Aliyah. Even if a family includes two *Sabras*, meaning Jews born in Israel, they still carry the traditions of their parents or grandparents who arrived in the land and required the support of others.

The Talmud teaches a rabbinic principle, *kol yisrael aravim zeh bazeh*, or "all Children of Israel are responsible for one another" (Babylonian Talmud, Shevuot 39a). While I am proud of our American Jewish community and our generous sense of philanthropy, in Israel, there is a real sense that we are all one family. There, we are all willing to help each other. It is for this reason that my wife and I could relax while our kids played at a park in Jerusalem, but we hovered around them while they played at a park in Los Angeles. In Los Angeles, we do not enjoy the same level of trust in strangers.

America is a society constructed around individual rights. Israel is a society designed around communal responsibility. All of these traits are contained within the two strands of the Jewish double helix. While it is possible to live an altruistic life focused entirely on helping others, I am not trying to set unreasonable or unrealistic expectations for American Jews.

I'm trying to encourage middlers to take one step closer to the collective responsibility of our people. Wherever you are on the rung, try to inch closer to the Israel strand. It is worthwhile.

It was a challenging year living in Israel. Living there is not the same as staying in a hotel. Our days were exhausting and lacked many American conveniences, but at the same time, our year in Israel was beautiful and one we will never forget.

My first trip to Israel following October 7 occurred in late November 2023. Six weeks after the horrific massacre, the Israel Defense Forces had entered Gaza in an effort to vanquish Hamas and rescue the hostages. Both stated goals proved difficult to achieve. We landed during a brief respite from battle, during the first period of hostage release in exchange for imprisoned terrorists. The mood was tentative and somber. Nobody knew what the exchange would bring.

As part of a group of Los Angeles rabbis, I arrived in Jerusalem in the early evening, and my eyes filled with tears. The normally bustling streets jammed with traffic lay quiet and barren. A smattering of cars drove through the neighborhoods, nothing like the experience I had of living there and witnessing the traffic jams—*pekakim*—of late-afternoon rush hour. I called home to try to describe the emptiness to my wife. The night air felt heavy.

We toured Kfar Aza, one of the kibbutzim devastated by the Hamas attack and left in ruin. We met with survivors who lost their friends, their homes, and, in some cases, even their hope. They were relocated to other communities throughout the middle of the country, separated from the rest of their community, from their known support systems. We sat as interested ambassadors of American Jewry and caring chaplains, and we listened to the outpouring of their anguish.

It was explained to us that Israel was founded on three fundamental trusts. On October 7, two of the three were profoundly broken. The first was the government. Not only did it lack readiness or a military strategy, but the government also felt absent to most citizens. The streets were filled with chaos and pain. Citizens stepped up to try to defend their friends. Soldiers answered WhatsApp messages from their comrades. The government was missing.

The second was the Israel Defense Forces. Unlike America, Israel maintains a mandatory draft, and the vast majority of citizens proudly serve as a matter of duty. Commonly understood to be the proudest and most significant institution in Israel, the strength of the IDF stands as a deterrent for Israel in its dangerous neighborhood. Anybody who has spent time in Israel understands the presence of the IDF in everyday life, as one sees soldiers on buses, at coffee shops, or on the beaches. The notion that it took the IDF between six and twelve hours to respond effectively remains one of the great unanswered questions concerning the massacre. When I speak privately to Israeli officials, they shrug and explain that they did not conceive of this kind of attack. The IDF was simply unprepared. It is hard to comprehend their absolute failure of imagination.

On the other hand, the third—and the only one—that endured was the bond between Israel and the Jewish people. Jews around Israel, and around the world, rallied in the face of the ensuing attack. *Kol yisrael aravim*—Israelis rushed toward the fighting to help their friends and family. American Jews mobilized institutions from federations to synagogues to provide information, to pledge money, and to lobby politicians to support the only Jewish state and the only liberal democracy in the region.

At the lowest moment, when Israel faced an existential threat, American Jews proved that we don't live on our own diaspora strand. We exist somewhere on the connecting rung between the two winding strands of the Jewish double helix. Indeed, we maintain the right to slide closer and farther to each pole as we see fit.

Previously understood as cultures heading in divergent directions, the response to October 7 invalidated that perception as a complete miscalculation. Any policy disagreement faded to the background as American Jews drew close to family across the world. We are family. The bonds of the double helix proved resilient.

—

The American strand of the Jewish double helix is weakening. As societies begin to decline, scapegoats are sought out. Jews understand this reality from thousands of years of experience. However, the American descent is not a military decline or a financial decline, but a moral erosion. One I believe we can fix.

We see the decline of our leadership evidenced in the hot and cold support for Israel in the months following October 7, our tenuous support for Ukraine against Russian aggression, and, in the future, our undoubtedly tepid support for Taiwan against China. This country no longer exudes the firm moral leadership it once did.

That moral ambiguity in our foreign policy bleeds into our domestic affairs as well. Only two decades after September 11, 2001, protestors in New York feel no shame in advocating for terror. From across the country, it looks as though New Yorkers seem to not mind.

On January 31, 2024, after mass pro-terror protests in Chicago, the city's mayor, Brandon Johnson, cast the tiebreaking vote in City Hall to pass a resolution calling for a humanitarian ceasefire in Gaza, which would not benefit Israel, not remove Hamas from power, nor demand the return of the hostages stolen from Israel and held in captivity in Gaza. After a reported 617 homicides and 2,450 shootings in Chicago in 2023, with an uptick in violent crimes, perhaps Chicago's mayor might consider a humanitarian ceasefire in Chicago first. The truth is that Chicago is home to a large Palestinian immigrant population. We cannot allow Palestinians in America to advocate for a biased agenda without the American Jewish community advocating for our own.

Indeed, our American Jewish organizational structures were totally unprepared for the sharp rise in Jew-hatred around urban centers, college campuses, and trusted media outlets. Many American Jewish organizations feel like relics meant to answer the priorities of a previous century.

The American Jewish community must adapt to the needs of a post-October 7 world. Our three key objectives should be supporting Israel, fighting Jew-hatred, and reestablishing moral clarity. There are organizations actively trying to gather support for Israel and attempting to stem the tide of Jew-hatred. They need more resources. For an American Jewish community divided by partisanship, acting with a false sense of security, and following a path of increased disassociation from synagogue life, moral clarity is an even more complex problem. Our sense of security has been shattered. Combatting antisemitism has begun. Now, we must look to the epicenters of Jewish morality, our houses of worship.

Moral clarity can be fostered only by a greater turn toward Jewish education and a renewed prioritization of synagogue life. All American Jewish children should receive a Jewish education that stresses the significance of peoplehood. This has, until now, not been stressed enough in formal and informal Jewish education, as David Gedzelman explained in the 2023 collection *Jewish Priorities*: "Jewish educational contexts for school-age children have been bereft of curricula or programming aimed at helping students understand the rich concept of Jewish peoplehood, explore textual bases for what the Jewish people is, or engage with the unique amalgam of the universal and the particular that is the fundamental Jewish proposition."

I grew up within a milieu of multiculturalism. For many Jews, that shifted toward a pure universalism that falsely claimed that all people were the same. All people should be treated the same, but all cultures are different. Cultural differences are beautiful and should be appreciated. For two decades, however, Tikkun Olam, or repairing the world in the form of social justice, has been championed as the core belief of the liberal denominations of American Judaism at the expense of other crucial principles. We need to return to learning the depth and breadth of the Torah, to prioritizing our shared sense of peoplehood with Israel and Jews everywhere, and to discussing God.

The prioritization of Tikkun Olam has betrayed the Jewish people. The world becomes outraged when most women are raped, when most babies are murdered, when most young people are taken hostage—but not, we have learned, when it happens to Jews. The world tolerates Jewish blood.

Jews must understand that we are different. Jews in America and Israel rely on one another for strength because we share a common destiny. The crucial bonds of the double helix must be explained and embedded within the souls of the next generation. October 7 should teach American Jews that peoplehood must stand now as our clear priority.

For American Jews, morality should emanate from our synagogue life. Synagogue membership and attendance afford the American Jewish community a break from a weeklong focus on the materialistic consumerism of the moment so that we can absorb the meaningful, eternal wisdom that has guided our people for millennia. Jewish values have steered us back from the precipice time and again to rebuild a bright future. Our tradition can do it again.

However, recent decades have seen the disintegration of community and the collapse of synagogue membership for a whole host of social reasons. Many of these social factors are elucidated in Robert Putnam's famous book *Bowling Alone: The Collapse and Revival of American Community*. We have to make the case for synagogue affiliation again. We must fight for a local community that meets regularly and studies the wisdom and merit of our ancient tradition. Synagogue offers a path toward rebuilding the moral foundation of our community here in America.

This argument assumes that synagogues will provide the kind of morality needed for this moment. There are many reasons, however, to question our rabbis' leadership and the seminaries that produce them. On May 17, 2024, two courageous rabbinical students wrote an essay in *The Forward* titled "Anti-Zionism Forced Us to Withdraw from Reconstructionist Rabbinical College." In the piece, Talia Werber and Steven Goldstein explain their brave withdrawal because they "experienced an increasingly vociferous anti-Zionism among the student body, the steady erosion of civil discourse and the seminary's inability to transmit the Jewish narrative to those it will ordain as future spiritual leaders of the Jewish people."

In truth, most seminaries do not teach the essential element of Zionism within Jewish identity today. In this moment of need for Israel, rabbinical schools have reduced the mandated time a student must spend in Israel. For the past several decades, seminaries have tolerated and even championed corrosive criticism of Israel as intellectual nuance and protected professors who continue to poison class after class of rabbis with anti-Israel rhetoric. Each seminary maintains its own faculty that encourages students to keep an open mind to the arguments of our adversaries, join social justice rallies by allying with advocates for our demise, and absolutely muddy the moral clarity required in this moment.

As seminaries abdicate their role in developing Zionism as a core principle for the American pulpit, programs and fellowships have been developed to help supplement the seminaries. Most notably, the Michael and Lisa Leffell Fellowship (associated with AIPAC) has emerged as a nonpartisan pro-Israel fellowship that teaches about the Zionist narrative and presents the current issues surrounding Israel's security. I am proud that I joined the second cohort of Leffell Fellows. Simply put, if a rabbinical candidate does not possess this fellowship line in their résumé, I would view it as a potential red flag and feel compelled to engage the candidate in a robust conversation about their education and beliefs concerning Israel.

American Jews know true moral leadership when they see it. It's time to demand it. We thirst to drink once again from the fountain of wisdom and morality. These sacred conversations belong in our sacred places. It is incumbent on those of us who know the taste of the fountain to help lead our friends and welcome our neighbors back into our sanctuaries.

~

It is crucial to remember that the foundational image of the Jewish double helix arrived in a dream. I'm not sure there is any previous indication in Genesis to think that Jacob could leave the land and bring his relationship with God along. I'm not sure that Jacob believed that God would renew the covenant with him while he ran away. We know from his reaction that he certainly did not expect a divinely inspired vision, "God is in this place, and I did not know!" (Gen. 28:16).

Another lesson learned from the episode is the merit of dreaming and imagination. Surely, few people would have imagined that after a century of decline and pogroms throughout Europe, Herzl's *The Jewish State* would be a prophecy accomplishable roughly fifty years after its authorship. Even after bringing Jews to return and build a nation, the founders of Israel argued all night on May 13, 1948, unsure of whether to declare Israel's establishment the next day.

These extraordinary accomplishments do not occur by studying reality. They manifest by following a dream beyond reality. Great moments in Jewish history stem from great moments of imagination. This is why revelation is usually expressed through a vision or a dream. Jacob dreams of the ladder. Moses approaches the Burning Bush. King David imagines national unity after a long tradition of tribal partitions. The early rabbis innovated a systematized oral tradition that centered around text. When we think beyond the accepted constraints, we can dream ourselves into a worthy tomorrow.

Our darkest moments happen when our leaders fail to imagine possibility.

CHAPTER 4

The Case for Dual Loyalty

By the end of the Book of Numbers, the Children of Israel have wandered for forty years in the wilderness. Our people are tired and hot, and it goes without saying that they're kvetchy. Then, they finally reach the wrong side of the Jordan River. Moses is excited to gaze across the river into the Promised Land, and it's at that moment that two out of the twelve tribes approach with a change of plans. The tribes of Reuven and Gad explain that they know that they're supposed to live inside the land, but they want to remain in the diaspora, in present-day Jordan. After forty years of walking in sand, they prefer the rich pastures of the land of Gilad.

Shocked, Moses asks them, "Will your brothers go to war inside the Land while you live here?" (Numbers 32:6). So, they make a deal. As long as the rest of the Jews were at war in the Promised Land and needed their help, the Jews living outside would be with them, shoulder to shoulder.

We are the inheritors of that ancient promise.

For most of our lives, Israel has not required that kind of help. Then, on October 7, we watched a scale of barbaric violence we had never witnessed, especially not beamed in real time to our cellphones and those of our children. In our *kish-kes,* we sensed the words of Moses: Will your brothers go to war inside the Land while you live here?

This year, we sensed the echo of that promise bubbling up from within our DNA, our double helix. Jews in Israel were in dire need of our help. And you know what? We showed up. We contributed money, we sent clothing, and many of us traveled there and volunteered. We made good on our ancient promise. We should be proud.

Why does that ancient promise between Moses and the tribes of the diaspora ring true today? Because it represents the underpinning of our peoplehood. American Jews must continue to embody the nature of that sacred biblical dual loyalty: We truly care about America as the home in which we live, and we truly care about Israel as our people's homeland. Teaching ourselves and our children to declare proudly our bond to Israel is a necessary repair for our souls as we endeavor to change the repeating cycles of diaspora.

When considering whether we can break the long, twisting arc of the repeating history of our diaspora, one must consider whether it is an eternally repeating pattern, baked into our nature, or whether it is a choice. All of the diasporic Jewish communities we construct bear a striking resemblance. The entirety of the diaspora is one large Anatevka. Like all great artistic masterpieces, *The Fiddler on the Roof* presented for us a great truth about the iconic shtetl experience. The shtetl from that musical—Anatevka—centered around its institutions: its home, its synagogue, its eatery, and its town square. We still build Jewish community according to this blueprint.

The shtetl existed between the two forces of tradition and change. Tevye symbolized the inclination to push to protect our tradition, while his daughters represented the forces pulling toward change. The first act of the musical glorifies and cherishes the shtetl experience. The pogrom at the midpoint changes the tone. Then, the characters contemplate their futures as the shtetl collapses around them. It fits perfectly into the biblical cycle of diasporic demise, set to marvelous music.

Every previous diaspora has been Anatevka. Egypt was Anatevka. Spain was Anatevka. Of course, Eastern European shtetl life was certainly Anatevka. The question remains: Is America another Anatevka?

On one hand, in almost every major city across North America, there is a highly concentrated Jewish community located in a cluster of suburbs. This reality allows for "Jewish geography" to be played rampantly and successfully. Our homes might be more extravagant, our social standing more esteemed, but active American Jews involved in organizational and synagogue life feel like a tight-knit community. In this way, it feels like we live in Anatevka.

On the other hand, our choice to live here in America provides a drastically different opportunity than did Anatevka. The American promise affords influence and power to any group that raises itself up in terms of education, affluence, and political involvement. This is the unique proposition that separates America from other diasporic experiences. As an American rabbi, an American adult, and especially as a father of American children, I take pride and comfort in the idea that our fundamental promise assures each generation that

America is always being shaped and reshaped. The United States began as a vision rooted in foundational principles and extends out as a vision open to negotiation. This access to power makes America feel very different than the hapless shtetl existence of Anatevka.

However, what if America is changing? In spite of every poll declaring that the vast majority of Americans support Israel, what if there is a quickening erosion within the largely moral American public? Notwithstanding overwhelming congressional support for American Jews, what if the campus protests in favor of anarchy, terror, and Jew-hatred symbolize a dimming of America's bright liberty? What if this tremor begins to repeat more frequently? What might the next tremor feel like?

This moment, today, affords us an incredible opportunity to break the chain of Anatevka. We have the benefit of history from which to learn. Thank goodness, we have not yet reached the end of *Fiddler*. Yes, we face all of the same threats of Anatevka. The external threats of Jew-hatred rage around us. Our internal inclinations to change ourselves and adapt to our surroundings are alive and well. Each of Tevye's daughters chooses a partner that represents a rejection of tradition in the form of social etiquette (Motel), political outlook (Perchik), and religious practice (Fyedka).

In *Mosaic*'s brilliantly reflective critique of *Fiddler on the Roof* titled "What's Wrong with *Fiddler on the Roof*," Ruth R. Wisse explains, "This illiberal form of liberalism, practiced by Jews as well as non-Jews, has always objected to the nexus of religion and peoplehood that has historically defined Jews and their civilization." In fact, it is time to recalibrate our moral compasses around religion and peoplehood as we never have before in our diaspora experience.

Our own Anatevka that began on the eastern bank of the Jordan River with Reuven and Gad and continued through most of our history can be broken only when we recognize a new ending to the story. Imagine a new version of *Fiddler on the Roof* in which American Jews show up to help. Dream of your arrival into the world of Shalom Aleichem to help lend strength and resources to the struggling shtetl community. Responsibility to our people demands our help. That is the only way to close the door on thousands of years in Anatevka.

We must reshape our American Jewish identity to rise above the anxieties and the restrictions of the shtetl and to honor our ancient promise to Moses. American Jews must prioritize our devotion—socially, financially, culturally, religiously—to the well-being of other Jews, in America and around the world, and especially Jewish people living in Israel.

The case for dual loyalty stems from a need to address the hierarchy of our identities. As American Jews, we need to place a greater priority on those two identities—our Americanism and our Judaism—above all other identities, such as political leaning, gender orientation, sexual preference, and socioeconomic class. For American Jews, this reorientation applies to our American identity as well as our Jewish identity.

Let us learn the lessons of history: That which is bad for Jews in America is bad for America. That which is good for Jews in America is also good for America.

I am not the first American Jewish leader to present this argument. Published in 1915, Louis D. Brandeis, who would go on to become the first Jewish US Supreme Court justice, penned an essay called "The Jewish Problem: How to Solve It." He wrote:

> There is no inconsistency between loyalty to America and loyalty to Jewry. The Jewish spirit, the product of our religion and experiences, is essentially modern and essentially American. Not since the destruction of the Temple have the Jews in spirit and in ideals been so fully in harmony with the noblest aspirations of the country in which they lived. America's fundamental law seeks to make real the brotherhood of man. That brotherhood became the Jewish fundamental law more than twenty-five hundred years ago. America's insistent demand in the twentieth century is for social justice. That also has been the Jews' striving for ages. Their affliction as well as their religion has prepared the Jews for effective democracy. Persecution broadened their sympathies; it trained them in patient endurance, in self-control, and in sacrifice. It made them think as well as suffer. It deepened the passion for righteousness. Indeed, loyalty to America demands rather that each American Jew become a Zionist. For only through the ennobling effect of its strivings can

we develop the best that is in us and give to this country the full benefit of our great inheritance. The Jewish spirit, so long preserved, the character developed by so many centuries of sacrifice, should be preserved and developed further, so that in America as elsewhere the sons of the race may in future live lives and do deeds worthy of their ancestors.

Those Zionist strivings that Brandeis mentions are now the Zionist reality of the State of Israel. He highlighted more than a century ago that an American Jewish prioritization of Jewish peoplehood and values adds depth and character to this country. He articulated why we must choose to be loyal to America *and* to the Jewish nation. That is the best way for us to live in America and carry our Jewish identity as a priority. We must choose a path forward with a greater collective responsibility for our people.

Those who resist this sense of peoplehood do so at their peril. American Jews already bear the brunt of Israel's decisions. The controversies of Israel's wars are imposed on us to defend. Outsiders recognize a truth that American Jews often overlook. Israel was established to be a Jewish state. We are Jews. We are all spiritually the Children of Israel.

Instead of being accused of these allegations by outsiders as disparaging, we should affirm them in a positive manner from the outset. We should all stand as extensions of the Jewish people, ambassadors for other Jews, ambassadors for Israel. We have maintained this foundational principle for a long time—*kol yisrael aravim zeh bazeh.*

The responsibility of Jews for other Jews is nothing new. We support one another because of our obligation to one another. Plus, we all bear a certainty that if we do not, nobody else will. As foreigners seemingly begin to distance themselves away from Israel, we must feel obligated to stand closer by her side. Peoplehood must stand clearly as our top priority.

It must be understood that peoplehood is not an optional facet of Jewish identity. It cannot be sacrificed on the altar of absolute loyalty to one's host nation and still be called Judaism. "Peoplehood" is, and has always been, at the absolute core of what being a Jew means.

Before we were a nation, we were a single family, a tribe consisting of the offspring of Abraham and Sarah, Isaac and Rebecca, and Jacob, Leah, and Rachel. Before we received the Torah at Mount Sinai, we were a people who had left Egypt together under Moses's leadership and gathered together beneath the mountain. Our sins were often collective sins—such as the Golden Calf—and our redemption was a collective redemption in the Promised Land. The entire Bible, from beginning to end, is a catalog of the voices, laws, foibles, teachings, songs, prophecies, and histories of a single people in relationship with our single God. Our story has always been a collective story, leading the ancient rabbis to teach that *kol yisrael aravim zeh bazeh*—our existence is collective, our mutual responsibility the basis for everything. Through thousands of years of exile, we maintained a single rabbinic culture, a single legal structure, and a single language—Hebrew, which we used when communicating with far-off Jewish communities, when praying, or when studying our holy texts.

The Case for Dual Loyalty

Commitment to fellow Jews everywhere is nonnegotiable. But alongside this we also felt a powerful, immutable commitment to returning one day to our homeland, the Land of Israel, the land promised to our forefather Abraham, the land that was worth forty years in the desert to reach, the land of the Bible. We maintained our single Holy Temple in Jerusalem for centuries, and when we were sent into exile, we never stopped praying for that return three times daily. We prayed in the direction of Jerusalem, and we bowed to God in that direction, so that we would never forget. Our leaders made multiple efforts to return there over the centuries. At weddings, we broke a glass to remember Jerusalem and sang the verse of Psalm 137, "If I forget thee, O Jerusalem, let me forget my right hand." When we comforted the bereaved sitting shiva, we said to them, "May the Lord comfort you among all of the other mourners of Zion and Jerusalem."

The establishment of Israel represents the funneling together of our two deepest loyalties that have burned inside us for thousands of years: To our people and to our land. Israel today represents both, and for this reason, it is a loyalty that no committed Jew can ever abandon.

We are a single people, and today the vast majority of Jews who do not live in America live in Israel. Israel is the nation that Jews built, the country and flag and army and industry that all exist to protect and defend Jewish life and the lives of all its citizens. Today our peoplehood and our Zionism stand as one.

For this reason, the second strand of the double helix is Israel. And we will always be loyal to it, for this is not a new loyalty, but merely the modern expression of our multi-millennial commitments to our people and homeland.

Today we are faced with a need to find new priorities that align with our ancient loyalties.

The need for this reprioritization has become true for American Jews as well as Israeli Jews. To survive the next set of geopolitical challenges, we will need to unite as Jews alongside one another in a way that has not yet materialized.

For Israeli Jews, the geopolitical forces that threaten its survival are clear. They mostly stem from Iran, and they take shape in the form of its proxies: Hamas, Hezbollah, the Islamic Jihad and other Palestinian factions, the Houthis of Yemen, and the militias of Iraq and Syria. Iran also pulls on the strings of puppet states, such as South Africa and all of Iran's allies, to deliver its international messages like prosecuting Israel for anything that resembles war. While Israel did not invent war, it feels like Israel is called time and again to defend the merits of a just defensive war for its survival.

Farther away, Israel faces threats from China and Russia, who oppose any entity that appears as allied with America. Israel and America are allied on multiple levels, and most important amongst them are the foundational principles of representative democracy, freedom from oppression, and a trusted legal system.

There are many articles, podcasts, and media personalities who discuss geopolitical forces in the Middle East. If you are not already familiar with Israel's history in an extraordinarily rough neighborhood, please go familiarize yourself with

Israel's narrative. But, for us, American Jews, how do we strategize to face our own oncoming tsunami of hate?

For American Jews, the "geopolitical forces" that undermine our existence take the form of a complete moral stupefaction. Certainly, China, Russia, Iran, Qatar, and North Korea are all trying to influence American society. We can see this through the forces from abroad wreaking havoc on our social media, traditional media, university faculty and policies, and political system. Many American Jews will read this argument and immediately find refuge in their own political preconception. This false attribution sounds like, "Of course there's foreign meddling in our elections. That's why we have to elect party X." Or, perhaps one might say, "To fight foreign investment in universities, we have to elect party Y." Both of these reactions reveal the prioritization of party politics over the peoplehood required in this moment.

For Jews to survive in America, we must begin to prioritize Jewish education, Jewish values, and Jewish narrative above the illiberal liberalism. All of the recent movements of identity politics, intersectionality, DEI initiatives, hyper-partisanship, and Marxist influences of the moment must be rejected. Taken to an extreme, these recent movements manifest in the pro-anarchist, pro-terror protests of 2023 and 2024.

None of it has ever aligned with Jewish values. It is not good for Jews, and it is not good for America.

Since these corrosive influences have taken up firm positions on the American Left, Jews must step away from this dangerous illiberal iteration of American progressivism toward the recognition that we belong to a greater narrative and a more crucial mission than the polarizing forces driving the American conversation at this moment.

Take as an example the most prestigious, emblematic university in America, perhaps in the world. On April 28, 2024, during the pro-Hamas, pro-terror encampment at Harvard University, students raised the Palestinian flag in a place where the American flag previously flew. At that moment, it wasn't only every Jew's responsibility, it was, in fact, every American's responsibility to storm the site and reverse it. But the Harvard intellectual elite didn't see it as the glaring symbol of the catastrophic collapse of our intellectual society. There is no more iconic indicator of a moral society's decay than the lowering of the greatest symbol for freedom and liberty that the world has ever known in favor of a symbol of permanent self-inflicted suffering, suicide vests, and barbaric terrorism. The Palestinian flags and the calls for intifada insult the memories of thousands of Americans who paid the ultimate sacrifice in Afghanistan and Iraq to protect our freedoms in a fight against global terror. It is no different than the way that Nazi symbols insult the memories of thousands of Americans who paid the ultimate sacrifice in Europe fighting Nazism and totalitarianism. That day in Cambridge, Massachusetts, signaled the absolute reversal of American values.

There will be readers who argue that the Palestinian flag does not represent terror. I would respond that in the context of the post-October 7 protests and encampments, that flag was utilized to stand with Hamas and all other Palestinian instruments fighting Israel. There are truly innocent Palestinian people who deserve a better future than their current reality, but none of them benefit from the extremist ideology of Hamas or its supporters throughout Gaza, and also on American college campuses. If they truly detest the brutal tyranny of Hamas, then they should fight against it. To bring dignity to the Palestinian people, they will one day be forced to excise the practice of terror and Jew-hating ideology from their schoolbooks and their society, and they will sit down across the table from Israel and negotiate a peaceful coexistence. This is a complex problem politically, but the solution begins with simple values and a working moral compass. None of this nuance was intended through the raising of the Palestinian flag at Harvard.

The moral corruption seen on college campuses reveals a complex problem too great for any singular political party to solve. This is a multilayered geopolitical problem. This is an American challenge. The hyper-partisanship of this moment prevents any prospect of resolution because every attempt by one party to galvanize opposition to any piece of the puzzle generates automatic sympathy by activists on the other side— as we have seen, for example, in the rise of far-right sympathy for Russia and opposition to arming Ukraine. Partisanship says: I don't care what's really a threat to America. I just know that if the other party opposes something, I should support it, and vice versa. We have to acknowledge the extremist ideology taking hold on college campuses as a threat to our American way of life. It is crucial to help America refocus on its traditional values and come together to meet the threat it now faces.

Just as this hyper-partisanship is a problem in America, it is a problem within the American Jewish community. Following the massacre and fallout of October 7, American Jews have vacillated between peoplehood and partisanship. They will argue, of course, that any significant change in this country must be processed through a partisan political apparatus. However, there are issues larger than partisan politics. Our bonds of peoplehood between Democratic Jews and Republican Jews must be stronger than partisan differences. American Jews must model this unbreakable bond for the rest of America.

American Jews must lead this country out of the toxic wasteland of hyper-partisanship. Our Talmudic texts teach us of the violence that necessarily results from prolonged enmity. The Sages teach us that the Second Temple and Jerusalem were destroyed by the Romans as a result of "needless hatred" among Jewish factions (Babylonian Talmud, Yoma 9b). For years, the rhetoric in this country has demonized members of the opposing political party. The political temperature here has reached dangerous levels. It is incumbent on us as American Jews to model civil decency as we recognize that there is more that unites us than divides us. No matter our political beliefs, we have surely lived through administrations that we opposed. Violence—whether in the form of physical attacks on minorities or destruction of the symbols that unite us as a nation—cannot be an acceptable reaction. The Bible commands us to "proclaim liberty throughout the land" (Lev. 25:10). It is our sacred responsibility as Americans and as Jews to do so. Just as that verse appears written in the Hebrew Bible and etched onto the Liberty Bell, so too do the foundational principles of our Jewish and American identities overlap.

Our dual loyalty does not mean that one undermines the other—to the contrary. Our ancient loyalty to our Jewish people is the bedrock on which our loyalty to America's promise of "life, liberty, and the pursuit of happiness" may most solidly be built. Our loyalty to that promise will help us lead the fight against all those who aim to dismantle the American experiment, and with it, the American dream—whether they are on the far left or far right. Just as Brandeis put it: *Loyalty to America demands that each American Jew become a Zionist.* But it goes further. When people in America burn the Israeli flag, when they march in support of the maiming and murder of Jews, when they attempt to cleanse the most influential institutions of Jews, they are assaulting the foundations of America as well.

The contrary is also true. Periods in which Jews have flourished here were also decades of prosperity and accomplishment for America.

For our sake, we must speak of our dual loyalty so that we are clear about our own red lines. I draw strength from other Jews. I live on the rung between the two strands with a great sense of loyalty to America and to Israel. This makes me a better Jew. This makes me a better American.

All Jews around this country should live with a sense of dual loyalty. We must take our identity and lift it above the confused national plane to a higher level that invokes the biblical call and the founding American vision of a better world based on the freedom and rights endowed by our Creator. My values are derived from a much higher source, the same source from which the American Founding Fathers derived theirs.

—

While I was writing my dissertation for my doctorate in religion at Claremont Graduate University, my advisor encouraged me to apply for a Fulbright. The Fulbright scholarship allows students to study and conduct their research abroad. During this process, American applicants try to find a host institution of higher learning in their desired foreign country. Then, through the application process, the applicants must make their case that their research can be uniquely enhanced through its new host location and respective institution.

Without much consideration, I saw the Fulbright as an excellent opportunity to spend more time in Israel. I constantly search for opportunities to spend time in Israel. Fortunately for me, the faculty at Bar-Ilan University in Ramat Gan, Israel, sponsored my application to continue my study of the Hebrew Bible. Sure enough, I received an acceptance and the great honor of a Fulbright scholarship to study at Bar-Ilan University.

Studying in the library at Bar-Ilan was an experience I will never forget. I was surrounded by the most esteemed Bible scholars in the world. Many of the professors expressed interest in my project and welcomed me into their offices for meetings and advisory sessions. The combination of studying biblical scholarship in academic Hebrew while listening to modern Hebrew bounce off the walls of the library was simply a dream come true.

It was at Bar-Ilan that I experienced a clarifying moment in my life. On my first day there, I struggled to find the office for foreign students to register for access to the library and all of the usual sorts of university bureaucracy. They asked for my Fulbright acceptance letter, my student visa, and my passport. The office administrator typed furiously to register me through what seemed like a thousand online forms. All of the forms on her computer screen appeared in Hebrew, and I had trouble keeping up as she scrolled through them at a rapid pace and entered my information in a fairly robotic manner. Occasionally, she would ask for the pronunciation of a word in English from one of my documents as she attempted to transliterate.

I realized she was creating my student identification card. I strained my neck to peer around her computer monitor and saw her enter my English name in transliterated Hebrew.

I looked at "Nolan Lebovitz" transliterated into Hebrew. It looked so odd. Like most American Jews, I have a Hebrew name given at birth—in my case, it's Natan, after my grandfather. Jewish tradition recognizes this as my "real" name, the name I am called up to the Torah by, the name on my *ketuba* or marriage contract. But now I was seeing for the first time my English name written like that, "Nolan" in Hebrew characters. I realized that this was going to be the first official document created for me in Hebrew in Israel. So, I stopped her and asked, "Can you use my Hebrew name for my student ID?"

"What do you mean your Hebrew name? I am writing your name in Hebrew."

I nodded, understanding her perspective, and then tried to make her understand my own. "Yes, I know. But, I have a Hebrew name. It's Natan. Instead of Nolan Lebovitz, on my student ID, can you please just write down Natan Lebovitz?"

She nodded, "Ahhh, now I understand. You love Israel?"

I nodded. I do love Israel.

"You want to change your name to a Hebrew name?" She handed me back my pile of paperwork. "Just go to the US embassy and request a change of name. They will change your passport, your papers, and then come back here once it's all done. Then, we can use your new Hebrew name."

A flash of panic overtook me. I did not want to head to the embassy or officially change my name in English. That Hebrew name is my name and always has been. So is my English name.

She rebuffed my arguments by pointing at my passport and all of my documentation. Why should I have to change my name suddenly for this one ID that I was supposed to carry in my phone?

I argued in circles with her for almost half an hour concerning this student identification that carries no authority whatsoever. I explained that I am Nolan, and I am Natan. I am both. She looked fascinated by my explanation, but I failed to change her mind.

What I had misconstrued as a meaningless document suddenly struck me as a pivotal moment in my life. Bar-Ilan University (like all Israeli bureaucracy, it turned out) would recognize my identity only as written on my passport, as approved by the US State Department. Why would I allow the State Department to characterize my identity *in the Jewish state?*

I thought back to Papa Nathan from whom I received my Hebrew name of Natan. I remembered his orphan upbringing, his subjugation at Auschwitz, and his pedaling in the bitter cold in Chicago. I also remembered his wisdom, courage, strength, and his sense of humor. I wanted to carry him with me in my doctoral research. I wanted to carry all of my grandparents with me.

Papa Nathan would have seen the argument over the student identification card as silly. He taught me that a love of Israel meant a responsibility for our loved ones there. For him, loving Israel meant loving Luba—a love I feel obligated to share with everyone I encounter in Israel and in America.

In the end, my Bar-Ilan student identification card read as my English name Nolan Lebovitz transliterated into Hebrew, just as the administrator insisted. I felt disappointed. That moment of bureaucratic failure pushed me to reconsider whether my passport truly represented me the way I'd like to be perceived in this world. It does not.

———

Several summers ago, I traveled to the Abraham Accords nations as part of the leadership of the Zionist Rabbinic Coalition, a nondenominational rabbinic group that aimed to support peers in standing with Israel. We traveled through the United Arab

Emirates and Bahrain and then ended our mission in Israel. The trip was eye-opening.

Never did I imagine that I would wake up in Abu Dhabi in the early morning, stand on my balcony in the heat, gaze at the Sheik Zayed Mosque, put on my tallit and tefillin for morning prayers, and pray westward toward Jerusalem. The glimpse of a peaceful Middle East filled with economic coexistence and religious tolerance inspired us all. The trip continues to inspire me, and I wait for the day I can lead a group there to taste the future.

We arrived in Dubai on a Friday, where we met with the Israel consul general before Shabbat. She explained to us that the Abraham Accords evolved over time. Not an obvious peace candidate from the outset, the Emiratis first felt comfortable with American Jewish businessmen who arrived to discuss foreign investment. Over time, the success of the partnerships allowed for an exploration of relationships with Israelis.

She smirked at our group, and she explained, "I'm not sure that you knew it, but you are some of Israel's best ambassadors."

That moment has remained with me. A member of the Israeli diplomatic corps recognized that American Jews serve as great ambassadors for Israel. I think she's right.

Whether intentional or not, all Jews serve as ambassadors for Israel. American Jews can travel to places Israelis cannot. We can explore greater possibilities. We can contribute to our collective imagination. When it comes to imagining a better future, the more, the better.

Following our experience of the aftermath of October 7 throughout the diaspora, and the stunning rise of Jew-hatred in America and throughout the world, I am often asked about our collective Jewish future in America. While I have no access to the ancient *urim* and *tumim*, the sacred stones the High Priest employed to interpret revelation, I have learned to apply our history, Judaic texts, my own family experience, and the time-tested wisdom of our tradition to the crisis of this moment.

On the whole, America will continue to be safe for Jews for a long time to come. We have many friends and allies. However, the urban centers that have traditionally welcomed immigrant populations and where Jews have established our communities might prove extraordinarily problematic. Consider New York and Los Angeles as key examples. Both cities are overwhelmingly liberal in their policies, politics, and culture. They're palpably secular. For a long time, those factors stood as positive signs for a location to build a Jewish community.

The two largest cities in America, in which the two largest American Jewish communities reside, continue to welcome other immigrant groups—in keeping with Jewish values to welcome the stranger. But today, this includes many foreigners who ardently hate Israel, and therefore hate Jews. This can be seen in the fervor of the pro-Hamas demonstrations on our streets and the pro-terror tent encampments at Columbia University, New York University, UCLA, and USC. With a noticeable absence of a dominant Christian culture recognizable in other parts of the country, other religious ideologies—including political extremism and Islamic fundamental-ism—can thrive. What made for fertile urban soil for Jewish immigrants to build businesses and synagogues now serves as fertile urban soil for the arrival of other groups and their own ideologies, who increasingly have a specific bone to pick with Jews.

The American Jewish community needs to pivot to consider our future. While I've witnessed a recent exodus of personal friends out of Los Angeles to Florida, Arizona, and Texas, for a host of policy reasons, we must ask ourselves why schools in largely conservative states with pronounced Christian cultures fared much better in pushing back against anti-American and anti-Israel demonstrations and rhetoric. The moral compass of those cultures recognized and under-stood the threat much more quickly than did secular cultures that purport to be more tolerant of each of us living according to our own rules. If the New York and Los Angeles communi-ties do not act to reverse the moral decay of the secular culture that surrounds them, Jewish families will begin transitioning out of these urban settings.

The first step toward this massive population redistribu-tion is already underway. For years now, Jewish enrollment in Ivy League schools has been declining—a process that has accelerated after October 7. In my own experience with Jewish students and parents of college-aged kids, I now hear much more about the University of Texas, University of Florida, University of Miami, Vanderbilt University, University of Wisconsin-Madison, and Tulane University.

There are two reasons for this. First, Jewish families feel more comfortable sending their children to campuses that enforce the safety of all students. While it is important to protect free speech as a fundamental American value, no student should be prevented or intimidated from walking through the center of campus or entering libraries or other campus buildings, as Jewish students were prevented in the spring of 2024 on elite campuses across America.

Second, as detailed recently in *Tablet Magazine*'s two brilliant articles, "The Vanishing" by Jacob Savage in March 2023 and "Ivy League Exodus" by Armin Rosen in April 2023, the eight prestigious Ivy League universities have long been scaling back their acceptance of Jews. Those institutions have come to prefer "diversity and inclusion" to the once-held American value of merit. As Jewish students in these elite-liberal settings feel less support and less community, they will likely feel more challenge toward their Jewish identity. Once the numbers dip below a certain point, they may rapidly disappear.

These two factors will encourage Jewish students to feel more comfortable in parts of the country where their parents might never have even set foot. The more comfortable the students feel in the southern states, the more likely they are to stay permanently. I know this lesson firsthand. Before I left Chicago for college, I informed my parents that I had no intention of staying in Los Angeles. Then, I became comfortable in Los Angeles, I aspired to work in Los Angeles, and I stayed.

If our children must begin venturing to parts of the country with a less-developed Jewish presence, they should carry with them a strong affinity for our peoplehood. In their pursuit of safer places for Jewish life, we cannot allow them to fall in love with new diasporic settings and new foreign communities and forget the reason for their arrival.

I know this from my own experience. When I arrived at college in Los Angeles, I noticed that the only state flag hung in dorm rooms was the Texas flag. I admired the pride of Texans, as I never considered hanging the Illinois flag. The closest I came to pride in Illinois was the Michael Jordan poster in my room.

This Texan pride is imbued in Texans from an early age. Texas raises its flag to the same height as the American flag. Symbols matter. The state covers itself with so many Texas flags that it's impossible to count that high. One cannot walk away from Texas without acknowledging its pride. Texas embodies an innate self-respect that we must emulate.

Our children must understand that the Israeli flag does not belong only in the sanctuaries of our synagogues. The Israeli flag belongs in their bedrooms and dorm rooms. It belongs around their shoulders. The flag of Israel should wave proudly in their hearts.

The same is true for the American flag. American Jewish children must be raised as patriots. I would love to see our personal houses flying the American flag and the Israeli flag. They don't only belong in our houses of worship.

Elite college campuses present for American Jews the ultimate challenge. As morally bankrupt professors and students try to shame our children away from American values and our brothers and sisters in Israel, we must do everything possible to infuse pride into our children's relationship with this country and our family in Israel.

Imagine a day when every American Jewish child leaves for college with a *mezuzah* to affix to their doorpost and American and Israeli flags to hang on their wall. We must condition ourselves to speak aloud our morality, and to enact our priorities in public, to live out our values for all to see. This is the only path forward to win the battle for the American Jewish soul.

———

A couple of years ago, I was enjoying a coffee with Randy Schoenberg, known as an accomplished attorney and a genealogy expert. His legal accomplishment was featured in the 2015 biographical film *Woman in Gold*. A proud grandson of the composer Arnold Schoenberg, he spends a great deal of effort tracing his family's roots throughout Europe. This process is captured in his documentary film *Fioretta*, in which I briefly appear.

During one of our conversations, he proudly told me how he had attained citizenship in Austria and had applied for citizenship in other countries as well. European countries were offering citizenship to Jews who could prove lineage back before the Shoah. Germany offers the same citizenship for those who can prove their family left due to the rise of the Third Reich. In 2015, Spain began offering citizenship to Jews who can exhibit their Sephardic ancestry and a connection to Spain. Now, many countries in the European Union offer citizenship based on ancestral ties.

Why would anybody want dual citizenship? Certainly, the notion broadens one's identity. To make oneself a dual citizen of America and Austria creates a far more global, cosmopolitan identity. Regular travel between countries broadens one's understanding of global issues from multiple perspectives. In addition, in a world of increasing economic globalization, dual citizenship allows for business to be conducted easier. It is always easier to relate to others when one is familiar with their customs. There are ideological and practical reasons to pursue a second passport.

For Jews, there is another reason. Many Jews play the game of "Where would we run?" Does any other religious, cultural, or ethnic group engage in this kind of conversation? Jews play this thought experiment based on the rise of Jew-hatred, the spread of tribalism, and the fear of massive political swings. Dual loyalty and dual citizenship with Israel would be an effort to finally acknowledge on paper what many of us have felt for a long time.

Why would Jews want to reattain citizenship in countries that tried to exterminate us? In one word: belonging. Randy Schoenberg feels connected to Austria due to his familial history. Many engage in ancestry to find out their family origins and discover where they came from. I would imagine that for Schoenberg, achieving dual citizenship in America and Austria recaptures a connection to previous generations.

I maintain a completely different perspective for myself and my family regarding Europe. My grandparents taught us that our family had no connection to their birthplaces, which were then Czechoslovakia and Poland. They used to tell stories from their youth about their antisemitic neighbors. They would remind us about how willingly and happily the Czechoslovakian and Polish civilians tormented them and proudly handed them and their families over to the Nazis. They were outsiders from birth. They were Jews. It is for this reason that I reject any notion that I am European or white. White Europeans rejected my family and murdered my relatives because I am, in fact, not one of them.

The blessings of America have confused our identity. Most American Jews feel comfortable in America. America is a melting pot of foreigners. It's the bright beacon of liberty that offers the light of freedom to the dark diaspora of oppression. Like so many other ethnic groups, Jews feel authentically American in our citizenship, culture, and language. I am a proud American.

My family is thoroughly American. And my family is thoroughly Jewish. We cheer for two teams in the Olympics. When we attend baseball games, we root for our team to win and for all the Jewish players on the other team also to play well. To aspire only to the status of authentic Americanism without Judaism is to repeat the mistakes of our collective past. The inclination to achieve dual citizenship is the right inclination. It is time for us to begin imagining our collective Jewish double helix as we consider our future.

Please remember, this book is intended for all of the middlers. There will be those who cannot imagine compromising their Americanism in any manner. This is the Jacob Blaustein position. They are stuck on the American strand of the double helix. There are many Jews who believe that the only place

Jews should live is in Israel. That is the Ben Gurion position. They are stuck on the Israel strand of the double helix. Most of us live on the rungs somewhere between those two poles. We feel a pull towards each side. We might even sense the tremors or hear the chants, but we're faithful to the promise of America. Still, we must inch closer to the middle.

Every American Jew should endeavor to live more closely to Israel. It is unrealistic for every American Jew to purchase an apartment in Israel as part of a plan ultimately to make Aliyah. Aliyah might be a wonderful byproduct of this argument that proves its success. Yet, if American Jews are trying to acquire a second citizenship and a second passport, then that second passport should certainly be Israel.

All American Jews should aspire to acquire Israeli citizenship.

This suggestion arrives as part of an entire menu of options that American Jews should consider at this point. All of us should bring our children to Israel from the earliest age possible to help craft their understanding of Israel based on the truth. This might be on a vacation in childhood, or it may be a gap year between high school and college. Gap-year programs are an amazingly effective tool to help children develop a sense of responsibility in a place where they will feel part of the collective.

In other words, for American Jews, Israel *should not be viewed as an escape*. It should be viewed as the source of meaning and character from which our children should draw pride. If you cannot ever imagine yourself as a dual citizen, try to move closer for your children's sake. Our children should have

Israeli friends, and they should know their way around Tel Aviv and Jerusalem.

For American Jews who do not believe America to be *galut*—exile—then we can certainly recognize Austria, Spain, and Germany as such. Our mission is not to move farther away into diaspora, but rather move closer between the two poles of Jewish existence.

In proposing this change, we must consider Israel's responsibility as well. It is not as easy to gain Israeli citizenship for American Jews (without moving there full-time) as it might be for those same American Jews to gain Austrian citizenship. This is the case for Schoenberg, who also believes that we should attain Israeli citizenship. Israel has much to gain from the prospect of millions more Jewish citizens. This would encourage millions of American Jews to spend more time in Israel and to raise their children believing that Israel is their home. In many ways, this additional Israeli passport for American Jews would simply confirm what many already feel. We have two homes. The State of Israel should take steps to simplify the process for global Jewry to gain citizenship.

This new chapter might also encourage our children to consider spending significantly more time in Israel for camp and gap-year programs and even participating in national service (*sherut leumi*) or IDF service. At a time when American colleges and universities feel unwelcoming and threatening to Jewish students, what could be a better alternative to college here than college there? Hebrew University, Tel Aviv University, Haifa University, Bar-Ilan University, Ben-Gurion University, the Technion, the Weizmann Institute, and

Reichman University are all world-renowned institutions of higher learning.

Dual citizens may even vote. There could be a threshold for the amount of time spent or national service for dual citizens to determine if one may vote. I visit Israel several times each year, and it feels crazy that Israeli citizens living in California who have not been to Israel in years can fly to Israel to vote in Israeli elections, and I respectfully observe. This would engage more Jews in Israeli national issues from a perspective of greater familiarity.

Plus, American Jews bring an appreciation of liberal democracy and governmental checks and balances that Israel desperately needs at this time. American Jews and Israel stand to gain from a stronger interest in one another. Dual citizenship is mutually beneficial.

—

To declare dual loyalty bears a challenge as well. The challenge exists on two levels. First, to live proudly as an American Jew who supports Israel bears with it consequences: socially and perhaps even professionally. To be an Israel-supporting American Jew is to be willing to lose friends—Jewish and non-Jewish—or to encounter hatred on social media. To support Israel outwardly means taking the risk that not all colleges or law firms or banks might want to accept it. Our Jewish identities need to be strengthened to withstand such challenges—just as our parents and grandparents withstood them in the 1940s and 1950s, when the exclusion of Jews from elite spaces was widespread and, in many cases, fully legal.

The second challenge concerns how we bolster our American Jewish soul to feel closer to our Israeli brothers and sisters. First, to prioritize peoplehood we should place greater emphasis on learning the language of our people: Hebrew. While American Jewish high-school kids learn to speak Spanish and French in one or two class periods per week, American Jews seem unable to speak Hebrew over the course of a nine-year day school education. We must prioritize and professionalize Hebrew-language education in our schools, in our synagogues, and in our lives.

Technology offers many more paths to learn Hebrew. There are tremendous apps one can use on their cell phone to learn for ten minutes each day. There are classes one can join from the comfort of their home. There are groups one can access to speak with others in Hebrew at multiple levels over Zoom.

Second, American Jews must visit Israel more often. Every American Jew should consider the ratio of their vacations concerning all other locations versus Israel. How can we steer ourselves to Israel more often? Meaning, if you currently visit Israel once every ten vacations, how might you make it once every five? Many American Jews complain to me that traveling to Israel is demanding. A trip to Israel requires a time commitment and a financial commitment. So does England and Italy and Japan. It's about priority. On a trip to Israel, our time and money are spent within our people. Every moment and every cent go toward strengthening the lives of our brothers and sisters in Israel and our own Jewish identity and that of our children.

Lastly, we should prioritize Israel, and the Jewish people more broadly, as we take political positions. I am not endorsing a single political party for American Jews. I am simply acknowledging that all elections are a series of choices. That process of choosing begins within, according to the priorities we hold in our hearts and minds. I know too many American Jews who prioritize many issues before what's best for Israel or the Jewish community. Again, how do we raise the interests of the Jewish state and people as a priority? If they are your third or fourth priority, how do we raise them to second or third? How might we raise them to the top of your list?

For if we take upon ourselves the responsibility of our people—there and here—we will not have to teach the merits of Israel. We will dress ourselves in the flag. We will attend and march at pro-Israel rallies. Some of us may even choose to live there.

Our children often don't notice the easy choices we make, the ones we take for granted. They notice, and learn from, those that require sacrifice.

Reshaping our Jewish identity to live as Americans and as Israelis will not be easy. It will be worthwhile. It will positively affect your own life and every life you touch.

~

To some extent, dual loyalty reflects the way most practicing Jews already practice. It would be a real challenge to find an American synagogue that doesn't display some association with Israel. Every day school teaches that Israel is our ancestral home, and some even culminate their sixth- or eighth-grade experience with a trip to Israel. It should be a safe assumption by any prospective student that Jewish high schools, college Hillels, and Jewish fraternities and sororities stand with Israel. To be Jewish in America today is to live in relationship with the State of Israel.

One might point to the radical young Jews who joined the pro-Hamas campus encampments as evidence that young American Jews do not stand with Israel. That is not my perspective. The young American Jews who stand with Hamas are a small minority, a reminder of the universalist, social-justice, Marxist self-loathing influence that opposes our sense of peoplehood. They will fade away over time from the epic narrative of our people.

Jewish education for young American Jews today must stress peoplehood and Jewish identity as top priorities. In doing so, the American and Israeli flags will continue to be presented side by side in their spaces.

In this October 8 world, we have an opportunity to forge a new path forward as to how we imagine Jewish citizenship. It begins by acknowledging the rampant, socially acceptable Jew-hatred that has permeated many public spaces in America and around the world. It begins by recognizing that many of the strategies that we employed as a people in thousands of years of diasporic experience have simply not worked. Our situation today provides a new framework to move ahead.

Jewish children throughout the world can all view themselves as prospective citizens of Israel. They should sense the enormous responsibility they maintain for one another. They should not fear any sort of national litmus test. American Jews enjoy tremendous privilege in this regard due to their American identity.

In Jacob's anxious moment of leaving the Promised Land, the ladder appeared. He saw the angels, and he heard the voice of God. "I am with you, I will protect you," God assured him, "and I will return you to this land" (Gen 28:15). God's message to Jacob, who also carries the name of Israel, was one of confidence in the diaspora. Meaning, wherever Israel headed, he was meant to feel assured that his unique relationship with God extended to any place he traveled.

As the inheritors of his covenant, we should carry that same confidence.

After all, we are Israel. Israel is us.

One might misconstrue this argument of dual loyalty for Jews alone. It's not. We are just the beginning. I believe Israel to be the worthiest democratic and just initiative in the world today that's under attack. One's decision to support Israel or to protest Israel is to immediately reveal to me the merits of one's character—regardless of whether one is Jewish.

All Americans should support and find loyalty to the cause of Jewish self-determination. The establishment of a modern Jewish nation-state in our ancestral homeland is the greatest affirmation that an exiled people can return to act as guardians of their own fate. Simply put, Israel's existence proves that dreams can, in fact, come true.

If one believes in liberty and democracy, in the values of the enlightened Western civilization, then one should believe in supporting its greatest outcome. The nationalist efforts of the Americans and the French did not face the same daunting odds as did the pioneers who built Israel. Yet, Israel succeeded in the same tradition of liberty and democracy.

Much of the world perceives each Jew to inhabit one strand or the other of the double helix. It's a trap. We must live in the space in between. American Jews today should all live as American and Israeli—as global Jews of a single people.

I am proudly loyal to America. I am proudly loyal to Israel. I hope you join me.

SOURCES

Mark K. Bauman. "The Blaustein-Ben-Gurion Agreement: A Milestone in Israel-Diaspora Relations." *Jewish Museum of Maryland*, April 5, 2018, https://jewishmuseummd.org/the-blaustein-ben-gurion-agreement-a-milestone-in-israel-diaspora-relations-part-1/.

Louis D. Brandeis. *The Jewish Problem: How to Solve It.* The Zionist Essays Publication Committee, 1915.

Shlomo M. Brody. *Ethics of Our Fighters.* Maggid, 2023.

Jonathan Chait. "Marjorie Taylor Greene Blamed Wildfires on Secret Jewish Space Laser." *New York Magazine*, January 28, 2021, https://nymag.com/intelligencer/article/marjorie-taylor-greene-qanon-wildfires-space-laser-rothschild-execute.html.

Amos Elon. *The Pity of It All: A Portrait of the German-Jewish Epoch, 1743–1933.* Picador, 2003.

Shia Kapos. "Ceasefire Vote Narrowly Passes Chicago City Council, Revealing Deep Divisions among Democrats." *Politico*, January 31, 2024, https://www.politico.com/news/2024/01/31/chicago-israel-hamas-ceasefire-resolution-00138950.

Franz Kobler. *Napoleon and the Jews.* Schocken Books, 1976.

David Gedzelman. "Teach the Idea of the Jewish People." In *Jewish Priorities: Sixty-Five Proposals for the Future of Our People,* edited by David Hazony. Wicked Son Books, 2023.

Daniel Gordis. *Israel: A Concise History of a Nation Reborn.* Ecco, 2016.

Theodor Herzl, *The Jewish State.* Dover Publications, 1946.

Jerusalem Post Staff. "American Jews: Over 51% Support Biden's Decision to Withhold Arms from Israel." *Jerusalem Post,* May 31, 2024, https://www.jpost.com/diaspora/article-804548.

JPS Hebrew-English Tanakh the Traditional Hebrew Text and the New JPS Translation. 2nd ed. of the New JPS translation. Jewish Publication Society, 1999.

Koren Talmud Bavli. Commentary by Rabbi Adin Even-Israel (Steinsaltz). Koren Publishers, 2012.

Matt Masterson. "Shootings, Homicides in Chicago Drop 13% in 2023 and Returned to Pre-Pandemic Levels, But Violence Numbers Remain Among Highest in Recent Decades." WTTW News, January 2, 2024, https://news.wttw.com/2024/01/02/shootings-homicides-chicago-drop-13-2023-and-returned-pre-pandemic-levels-violence.

Dr. Mordecai Naor. *The Friday That Changed Destiny 5th Iyar 5708 (May 14, 1948): The Drama of the Establishment of the State of Israel.* Yehuda Dekel Library and Society for the Preservation of Israel Heritage Sites, 2014.

Ewan Palmer. "Rashida Tlaib's Palestinian Flag Sparks Call for Congress Ban." *Newsweek,* October 10, 2023, https://www.newsweek.com/rashida-tlaib-palestine-flag-office-hamas-ban-1833320.

Tamar Pileggi. "Obama: Iran could be a 'very successful regional power.'" *The Times of Israel,* December 29, 2014, https://www.timesofisrael.com/obama-iran-could-be-a-very-successful-regional-power/.

Politico Staff. "Full Text: Trump's Comments on White Supremacists, 'Alt-Left' in Charlottesville." *Politico,* August 15, 2017, https://www.politico.com/story/2017/08/15/full-text-trump-comments-white-supremacists-alt-left-transcript-241662.

Robert Putnam. *Bowling Alone: The Collapse and Revival of American Community.* Touchstone Books, 2001.

"Reform Judaism: The Pittsburgh Platform (November 1885)." Jewish Virtual Library, https://www.jewishvirtuallibrary.org/the-pittsburgh-platform.

Armin Rosen. "Ivy League Exodus." *Tablet Magazine,* April 18, 2023, https://www.tabletmag.com/sections/arts-letters/articles/ivy-league-exodus.

Jacob Savage. "The Vanishing." *Tablet Magazine,* February 28, 2023. https://www.tabletmag.com/sections/news/articles/the-vanishing.

"Jewish Population Rises to 15.3 Million Worldwide, with Over 7 Million Residing in Israel." Jewish Agency, September 25, 2022, https://www.jewishagency.org/jewish-population-rises-to-15-3-million-worldwide-with-over-7-million-residing-in-israel/

Rikki Schlott. "Wealthy Jewish Families Are Rejecting the Ivy League for 'Plan B' Schools." *New York Post*, November 27, 2023, https://nypost.com/2023/11/27/news/wealthy-jewish-families-reject-ivy-league-for-plan-b-schools/.

E. Randol Schoenberg. "Citizenship, Nationalism and How to Solve Part of the Israel-Palestinian Problem." Schoenblog.com, March 13, 2019, https://schoenblog.com/?p=1796.

Simon Schwarzfuchs. *Napoleon, the Jews, and the Sanhedrin*. Routledge & Kegan Paul Ltd, 1979.

James Traub. "The New Israel Lobby." *The New York Times*, September 9, 2009, https://www.nytimes.com/2009/09/13/magazine/13JStreet-t.html.

Gil Troy. "Fighting against Antisemitism Effectively: Non-Jews Should Engage Too." *Jerusalem Post*, June 11, 2024, https://www.jpost.com/opinion/article-805780.

Gil Troy. "National Insecurity: The Case for Jonathan Pollard." *Tablet Magazine*, November 16, 2010, https://www.tablet-mag.com/sections/news/articles/national-insecurity.

Gil Troy. *The Zionist Ideas: Visions for the Jewish Homeland—Then, Now, Tomorrow*. The Jewish Publication Society, 2018.

Gil Troy. *Theodor Herzl: The Collected Zionist Writings and Addresses of Israel's Founder, Whose Relentless Drive Enabled the Establishment of the State of Israel.* The Library of the Jewish People, 2022.

George Washington. "From George Washington to the Hebrew Congregation in Newport, Rhode Island, 18 August 1790." The National Archives: Founders Online, https://founders. archives.gov/documents/Washington/05-06-02-0135.

Bari Weiss. "Bari Weiss: The Holiday from History Is Over." The Free Press, March 12, 2024, https://www.thefp.com/p/ bari-weiss-the-holiday-from-history-is-over.

Talia Werber and Steven Goldstein. "Anti-Zionism Forced Us to Withdraw from Reconstructionist Rabbinical College." *Forward,* May 17, 2024, https://forward.com/opinion/ 614347/anti-zionism-reconstructionist-rrc-rabbis/.

Ruth R. Wisse. "What's Wrong with 'Fiddler on the Roof.'" *Mosaic Magazine,* June 18, 2014, https://mosaicmagazine. com/observation/uncategorized/2014/06/whats-wrong-with-fiddler-on-the-roof/.

All English translations of Hebrew and Aramaic texts have been informed by cited works but are ultimately the author's own.

ACKNOWLEDGMENTS

David Hazony deserves a great deal of credit for editing this book. After working together on my essay for *Jewish Priorities*, he is more than merely a copy editor. He is a thought partner and a friend. I always look forward to meeting him for a cup of coffee in Jerusalem.

I will always be grateful to Adam Bellow for publishing this work. In a world in which most Jewish publishing houses have folded, he has persevered to maintain our tradition of Jewish public thought. The American Jewish community is better off because of his passion for the written word.

I also want to acknowledge Valley Beth Shalom and its lay leadership for all of its support. This book bridges the terms of two presidents and many directors of the board. To all of them, I owe a sense of thanks for understanding my passion for writing and my passion for Israel. This book is the culmination of both.

To everyone who read a draft of this book or listened to me describe a section, thank you for all of your patience and support.

ABOUT THE AUTHOR

Photo by Shlomo Ben-Avi

Nolan Lebovitz serves as the senior rabbi at Valley Beth Shalom in Encino, California, and sits on the executive board of the Zionist Rabbinic Coalition. In 2024, he earned his PhD from Claremont Graduate University's Religion Department, focusing on his study of the Hebrew Bible. That same year, he accepted a position as an adjunct fellow at the Z3 Institute, which is part of the Palo Alto-based Z3 Project that is helping develop the next stage of Jewish life. A Fulbright scholar, Lebovitz spent time in 2023 studying at Bar-Ilan University in Israel. He wrote and directed two documentaries: *Roadmap Jerusalem* in 2018 and *Roadmap Genesis* in 2015. He was ordained with a master's degree from the American Jewish University's Ziegler School of Rabbinic Studies in 2016. He earned his BA from the USC School of Cinema-Television. A grandson of four survivors of the Shoah, he carries an obligation to teach the lessons of our past in hopes that we can chart a new, more hopeful course forward for our collective Jewish future.

Made in the USA
Las Vegas, NV
08 January 2025

16038948R00085